# From Pie Stand to Icon:
# The 100-Year History of
# *The Cherry Hut*

## Beulah, Michigan

# From Pie Stand to Icon: The 100-Year History of

# *The Cherry Hut*

## Beulah, Michigan

## Claudia C. Breland

### Introduction by
### Michael Stern

MISSION POINT PRESS

Published by Mission Point Press
2554 Chandler Rd.
Traverse City, MI 49696
(231) 421-9513
www.MissionPointPress.com

Painting on cover by Casey Crandon, 2004
Book design by Sarah Meiers

ISBN: 978-1-954786-97-4
Library of Congress Control Number: 2022908063

Printed in the United States of America

This history is dedicated to the
staff members and customers
who made The Cherry Hut
what it is today.

# Contents

# Introduction

**When I grew up in northern Illinois,** my family's ritual summer vacation was a trip around Lake Michigan. We'd head north into Wisconsin for bratwurst and butter burgers, for a fish boil in Door County, and for Cornish pasties in Michigan's Upper Peninsula. Across the Straits of Mackinac, we stopped for fudge on Mackinac Island.

The pace slowed and sweetened as we cruised onto M-119, a winding two-lane road that once was a Chippewa footpath and now is known as the Tunnel of Trees. Oak, maple, and pine grow thick above a forest floor of spring trillium, forming a canopy over the road through which light sprinkles down like pixie dust. Beyond that, Highway 31 heads towards Grand Traverse Bay and the cherry orchards of Benzie County.

In spring, the landscape is fluffy pink with hills of blossoming cherry trees; starting in June, roadside stands sell bags of washed cherries—dark, firm, bursting with juice, ready to eat as you drive. When Memorial Day comes, The Cherry Hut of Beulah opens its doors and starts serving cherry pie.

To fork up a piece of Cherry Hut's legendary pie is to know the unique charisma of the cherry. After all, cherries aren't just another fruit. They are so wonderful that a happy life is described as a bowl of them. Many years ago, Leonard Case, then proprietor of The Cherry Hut, told us, "The cherry is unique. It is so pretty, round, and red; the sight of cherries on their stems makes people happy like no other fruit."

What's striking about northern Michigan's favorite summer fruit, and what makes Cherry Hut pies extraordinary, is that sweetness is a secondary quality. Yes, of course the pie is sweet; but beyond sweet, it is tart and exciting.

Mr. Case started his career at The Cherry Hut when he was a high school sophomore. His job then was making cherry jelly for James and Dorothy Kraker, who originally opened their place as a roadside stand in 1922. It wasn't a restaurant then. It gained renown among travelers for pies made from cherries grown on the Kraker family's trees. Leonard Case never left the business, and in 1959, he bought the place. Today it remains a Case family enterprise, now helmed by Leonard's son, Andy.

Of course, The Cherry Hut has changed over the years. What started as a farm stand now is a full-service restaurant. The price of a slice of pie has gone up from the 20 cents my father paid for it in the 1950s. You now can mail-order Cherry Hut cherry products year-round.

When we included The Cherry Hut as one of the great regional restaurants in the original edition of our guide book *Roadfood* in 1977, we marveled that a single slice was one-quarter of an entire pie. If you got it à la mode, it came topped with about a half a pint of ice cream. Joyously, that's still true.

Of the 400 restaurants listed in that first edition of *Roadfood*, not all retain the personality they had when we first described them as essential stops for a true taste of America. Some have bitten the dust. Others have lost the way or gotten too fancy to be the sort of unique personal experience that makes a food-focused road trip so much fun. The Cherry Hut has remained a recommended stop in every one of the ten editions of the *Roadfood* guidebook published since the 1970s. It now is a highlight at Roadfood.com.

We're sometimes asked to pick a single restaurant from each state to represent that state's most delicious contribution to American gastronomy. When it comes to Michigan, the choice is easy. Of course, it's The Cherry Hut.

And when we write an article about The Cherry Hut, can there be any doubt that we'll include a picture of Cherry Jerry, The Cheery Cherry Pie-Faced Boy? This cartoon mascot with his perfectly round, bright red pie-face has come to symbolize Benzie County cherries to generations of travelers. Now a century old, The Cherry Hut itself is as fundamental a feature of the landscape as the orchards themselves.

— *Michael Stern, Roadfood.com*

# How It All Began

**The Cherry Hut story begins with Dorothy Rogers,** who was born in 1888 in Milwaukee, Wisconsin. There she spent her first years with her widowed father, Augustus, and older siblings Althea and Augustus (A.J.).[1] Dorothy's father remarried in 1902 to Jane Bowen Passmore, who survived him by many years.[2] And in 1904, the *Benzie Banner* published a small notice that "Mr. A.J. Rogers of Milwaukee, Wis., has rented the cottages of G.C. Hopkins and will spend the summer there."[3] Dorothy's father, Augustus Rogers, bought 80 acres on the North Shore of Crystal Lake where he took his family to camp. Sadly, he died in 1907. Thereafter, Jane Passmore Rogers and her stepchildren A.J., Althea (known as "Dautsie") and Dorothy made regular trips across Lake Michigan from Milwaukee to Beulah for the summer. Several years later, it was noted that "Miss Dorothy Rogers will teach at South Frankfort this year."[4] She had previously received a master's degree in bacteriology.[5]

James Lewis (J.L.) Kraker was born in New York in 1889, and in 1900 was living in Manhattan with his widowed mother Sophia and older sister Annabel.[6] He graduated from Cornell University in 1912, studying agricultural economics.[7] After graduating he went to work for Mulford Colloidal Laboratory in Philadelphia, which is where he met Dorothy Rogers.[8] In August of 1917, the *Benzie Banner* announced their marriage.[9] By 1920 they were living on Orchard Street in Benzonia, and in 1921 they purchased 80 acres of land on the north shore of Crystal Lake.[10]

The previous owner, Percy Reed, had planted "several hundred cherry trees" in 1911 with the help of his grown sons Maurice and Orville.[11]

In January 1919 J.L. Kraker was appointed Agricultural Agent for Benzie County.[12] The year after J.L. and Dorothy Kraker bought the land and cherry orchard on the north shore of Crystal Lake, they began selling cherry pies from their roadside stand on the corner of Warren Road and North Shore Drive.

On April 1st, 1911, we moved a few household goods over to our farm home and commenced operations.  The boys, Maurice and Orville, took hold and we set out several hundred  cherry trees

Excerpt from Percy Reed's autobiography, written in 1947

Percy Reed's farm on the north shore of Crystal Lake, circa 1911

Received for Record this _____ 11th _____ day of _____ April _____ A. D. 19 21 _____, at _____ o'clock _____ M.

_____ Edwin S. Heine _____ Register of Deeds.

_____ Deputy.

Percy A. Reed deed
TO

James L. Kraker wf

## This Indenture

Made this _____ 11th _____ day of _____ April _____

in the year of our Lord one thousand nine hundred and _____ twenty one _____

BETWEEN _____ Percy A Reed and Mary A. Reed, his wife, of Benzie, Mich _____

_____ of the first part,

and _____ James L. Kraker and Dorothy R. Kraker, husband & wife, jointly, _____

_____ of the second part,

WITNESSETH, That the said parties of the first part, for and in consideration of the sum of _____ One Dollar and other valuable Consideration _____ Dollars,

to _____ them _____ in hand paid by the said part ies of the second part, the receipt whereof is hereby confessed and acknowledged, do _____ by these presents, grant, bargain, sell, remise, release, alien and confirm unto the said part ies of the second part, and _____ their _____ heirs and assigns, FOREVER, ALL _____ that _____ certain piece or parcel of land situate and being in the _____ Township _____ of _____ Benzonia _____

County of Benzie, and State of Michigan, _____ and described as follows, to wit :

The East half (E½) of the North West quarter (NW¼) of Section Nine (9) Town Twenty one (the) North Range Fifteen (15) West and Containing 80 acres more or less according to the Government Survey

U. S. I. R.
$ ___
4/11/21
Benz.

Together with all and Singular, the hereditaments and appurtenances thereunto belonging, or in anywise appertaining; To Have and to Hold the said premises, as herein described, with the appurtenances, unto the said part ies of the second part, and to _____ their _____ heirs and assigns FOREVER. And the said _____ Percy A Reed & Mary A Reed _____

part ies of the first part, for _____ themselves their _____ heirs,

executors, and _____ administrators, do _____ covenant, grant, bargain and agree to and with the said part ies of the second part _____ their _____ heirs and assigns, that at the time of the ensealing and delivery of these presents _____ they are _____ well seized of the above granted premises IN FEE SIMPLE; that they are free from all incumbrances whatever except a purchase price mortgage given by James L. Kraker & wife

and that _____ they _____ will, and _____ their _____ heirs, executors, _____ administrators, _____ shall Warrant and Defend the same against all lawful claims whatsoever except as to said purchase price mortgage

In Witness Whereof, The said part ies of the _____ first part, ha ve hereunto set _____ their _____ hands and seal S the day and year first above written.

Signed, Sealed and Delivered in Presence of

_____ Giles Seel _____

_____ H B Woods _____

Percy A Reed　[L.S.]
Mary A Reed　[L.S.]
_____　[L.S.]
_____　[L.S.]

The 1921 deed for the Kraker's purchase of the cherry orchard on the north shore of Crystal Lake.

# The 1920s

**Highlights of the Decade:**

- **1921:** J.L. Kraker bought land with several hundred cherry trees from Percy Reed
- **1922:** J.L. and Dorothy Kraker set up roadside stand on the north shore to sell cherry pies
- **1922:** Dorothy's brother A.J. Rogers became president of the Benzie County Farm Bureau and along with J.L. Kraker and James Dymond founded the Michigan Cherry Growers Association
- **1925:** National Cherry Festival began in Traverse City
- **1926:** 1500 cherry pies were sold during summer season
- **1928:** Cherry Hut opened 2nd location on US 31 in Benzonia
- **1929:** Cherry Hut in Traverse City opened

**When the Krakers settled on their farmland,** Dorothy thought of putting a stand down by Orchard Corners on North Shore Drive and selling cherries. Her husband suggested that people would be more likely to buy cherry pies.[13]

As Dorothy told the *Farm Journal* reporter, Virginia Brown,

> The first day we didn't have a customer. The second day, two stopped. So we had a council of war. We *had* to save our stand. We decided to put up signs along the road saying 'Cherry Pie—One Mile' and 'Cherry Pie—½ Mile.'
>
> Not long afterward a Grand Rapids newspaper published a picture of our sign and said, 'A one-mile pie is *some* pie!' That advertised us, and we were pretty well started.

A customer pulls in front of the cherry pie roadside stand, opened in 1922.

New beginnings: Dorothy Kraker awaits customers at her new pie stand.

This Cherry Hut photo was taken in 1925.

With the headline, "Northwest Region Plans Cherry Fete," the *Detroit Free Press* announced the first Traverse City Cherry Festival to be held in 1925, proclaiming that "this section of Michigan should honor the cherry as much as Holland honors the tulip and California the rose."[14] Subsequent newspapers outlined plans for the festival, which would include the "Blessing of the Blossoms" in spring, a parade, a pageant and the crowning of a cherry queen.[15] This festival also started the tradition of sending a cherry pie to the President of the United States.[16]

It only took a couple of years before Cherry Hut cherry pies became very popular. The first advertisement was published in the *Benzie Banner* in 1925, and in 1926 Dorothy Kraker wrote an article for *The Rural New Yorker* titled "Selling Cherries in Pie Packages":

*On the north shore road of beautiful Crystal Lake, in Benzie County, is a little white shack, nestled under the bluff with a huge white birch hanging over it. A quarter of a mile down the road on either side of this spot, the tourist, vacationer or native has his eye attracted by a neat red and white sign announcing, "Cherry Pie – ¼ Mile." So when the large red and white sign over the little 10x10 shack reads "The Cherry Hut," and a most appetizing smell of baking issues forth, the tourist has already slowed up, and it is usually the man or men of the party who this time wishes to stop. A red and white striped awning protects the hut from the sun, and under it is a red bench. Three windows are hung with cherry red curtains. The counter usually has some red or white flowers on it, surrounded by cherry pies, covered with waxed paper as a protection against road dust. A few of the pies are small, but most of them are regular farmer-sized pies.[17]*

Three Cherry Hut girls take time out to pose for a photo.

In this article, Dorothy goes on to describe the humble setup with which they began: a three-burner oil stove, an icebox, shelves for dishes and pie plates, and an old lard pail that's used as a flour bin. Daily sales of cherry pies averaged about 25, and they were known to run out before they closed up shop, taking orders for the following day. The Cherry Hut also sold eggs from their 200 White Leghorn hens, cherryade and black sweet cherries. Decades later, the first Cherry Hut was described as "a whitewashed chicken coop."[18]

In 1925, the previous year, The Cherry Hut sold over 1,000 pies during the summer season. The average cost of ingredients per pie was about eighteen cents, and the pies were sold for forty cents. The Krakers also worked with the local canning factory, the Grand Traverse Packing Company, to provide customers with cherries to take home to make their own pies.

Another pivotal event in the area's—and Cherry Hut's—history was the formation of the Cherry Growers Association. As early as 1920 fruit growers were meeting to discuss common problems.[19] In April 1922, the *Benzie Banner* announced that several local cherry growers met, including A.J. Rogers, James Dymond and J.L. Kraker of Beulah, along with other growers from Traverse City and Bear Lake.[20] The purpose of the meeting was to discuss pooling the cherry harvests, and to install modern processing technology such as a pitting station and possibilities for putting the cherries into cold storage rather than canning them. This would enable the Association to hold the cherries to get the best prices. In June 1922, A.J. Rogers, Farm Bureau president, organized a meeting to discuss ways to market cherries in Detroit, and on the new method of packing cherries in lugs rather than sixteen-quart crates.[21] And in 1924, a long article on the front page of the *Benzie Banner* announced J. L. Kraker's resignation from the Farm Bureau, because "my farm interest in this county needs my entire attention and I expect to devote my time to this work."[22]

Dorothy Kraker and Marjorie Case smile for the camera.

Not long afterwards, a homespun poem appeared in the local papers:

Cherries ripe, Ripe, RIPE, I cry
Full and Fair ones—come and buy[23]

A poetic ad for ripe cherries appears in the
*Benzie Banner*.

News of The Cherry Hut was spreading to other parts of the state; in November 1926, the *Grand Rapids Press* proclaimed that during the summer season Mrs. Kraker had sold 1,500 cherry pies and had to employ two assistants to keep up with the demand.[24]

In 1929, an article in the *Traverse City Record-Eagle* announced that J.L. Kraker was opening another Cherry Hut in Traverse City at Barlow and East Front streets to be staffed by Miss Jessie Small and Miss Marion Whitney.[25] This was following the opening of the second Cherry Hut outlet the year before in Benzonia, "opposite the Benzonia Garage."[26] This is the same location where the Benzonia Cherry Hut's jam kitchen stands today.

The following year, 1930, would see even more expansion. The Krakers' two children, Jimmy and Althea, were old enough to help out, and the Beulah Cherry Hut found a new location to call home.

The Cherry Hut expands to a new location.

# CHERRY PIES AT A ROADSIDE HUT

J. L. Kraker, Beulah fruit grower, has opened his Traverse City cherry hut, which will dispense cherry pies through the season in the same manner and number as the two cherry huts he has operated at Beulah and Benzonia for the past several seasons.

Miss Jessie Small, who has been employed by Mr. Kraker in previous years, and Miss Marion Whitney of Traverse City are in charge of the hut, which is located at Barlow and E. Front streets.

The *Grand Rapids Press* announces the new Cherry Hut in downtown Traverse City.

With baskets on their arms, young men gather to pick cherries.

**Claudia C. Breland**

Women gather for the hard work of pitting cherries.

## Celebrating Our Staff: 1920s

Betty Carr

Jean Carr

Elinor Case

Margaret Case

Marjorie Case

Dorothy Kraker

Ruth Lyberg

Jessie Small

Chestina Sprout

Marion Whitney

Catherine Woodward

# The 1930s

## Highlights of the Decade:

- **1930:** Cherry Hut opened a year-round outlet in the Chicago Loop District
- **1932:** Main Street in Beulah was paved
- **1935:** North Shore Drive in Beulah was paved
- **1935:** Cherry Hut was relocated to its present location on US 31 in Beulah
- **1937:** Beulah marked successful resort season

In 1930, The Cherry Hut opened in the Chicago Loop District.

**Even as the Great Depression began,** The Cherry Hut kept expanding. In June 1930 the Fruit Growers Association, made up of cherry growers in Michigan and Wisconsin, leased space in the Chicago Loop district. One years' rent was $3,600 (about $60,000 in today's dollars), and the intent was to show how frozen cherries were more versatile than they might seem and could be used in several different ways.[27] Dorothy Kraker and Marjorie Case traveled to Chicago to staff the new location.[28] This location operated through at least 1932.[29] At the end of their first season in Chicago, Dorothy and Marjorie decided they would return to Frankfort by canoeing along the shore of Lake Michigan, some 250 miles. They had to quit after just a few days, but only because it rained the whole time![30]

A 1930s Cherry Hut menu features sandwiches, beverages, and cherry-inspired desserts (of course!).

MENU
The Cherry Hut :

SANDWICHES—
    Sliced Turkey.................................50
    Turkey Salad...............................40
    Baked Ham.................................35
    Ham and Cheese........................45
    Toasted Cheese..........................25
    Egg Salad...................................25
    Cherry Jelly................................15
Turkey Salad Plate with Rolls...........75
Homemade Soup (with Croutons).....25

DESSERTS—
    Cherry Pie...................................20
    Pie a la mode..............................25
    Cherry Sundae............................20
    Cherry or Vanilla Ice Cream.........10

BEVERAGES—
    Coffee or Tea..............................05
    Milk............................................10
    Cherry Ade.................................10
    Iced Tea or Coffee.......................10

Whole Cherry Pie (To take out)......75

ASK ABOUT OUR JAMS AND JELLIES——
    CONSIDER OUR "ASSORTMENT-OF-THE-MONTH"

The saying "imitation is the sincerest form of flattery" was illustrated by the fact that fruit growers in Traverse City "have borrowed from Mr. and Mrs. Kraker of Benzie County their idea of the Kraker cherry pie huts and have established like huts in many cities, going as far as Philadelphia..."[31]

Progress showed up on the home front in 1932, when the paving of Main Street in Beulah was approved by state highway administrators in Lansing.[32] In the same newspaper, bread was advertised at six cents a loaf.[33] By 1934, summer visitors were enticed by the showing of talking pictures in Beulah Park, every Wednesday.[34]

In 1935, The Cherry Hut relocated to its present location on US 31 in Beulah.[35] In this location, the Krakers could expand services by adding several round tables shaded by umbrellas for outdoor dining.[36] The menu had expanded a little, and was now printed on red cardboard, illustrated with stick figures drawn by J.L. Kraker.

J.L. Kraker probably leased the land from Martin Trapp, who had established a well-known "muck" farm here, known across the state for its celery and onions.[37]

Martin came to northern Michigan from the Netherlands and bought the land along the east side of US 31 and farther east of Beulah, in order to establish his vegetable gardens.[38] He would line this section of land with gladiolas every spring. At the time of the land transfer in 1935, Martin probably never imagined that four of his granddaughters would work at The Cherry Hut, one of them becoming the National Cherry Queen!

Martin and Mary Trapp pose with their granddaughter Mary Lonn Trapp, who was crowned a National Cherry Queen.

Lewis Kraker and Martin Trapp shared a very close friendship for much of their lives, as Lewis replaced Martin as Farm Bureau Agent in 1919 and lived across the street from the jam kitchen in the 1930s and '40s. That's why Martin was so willing to invite Lewis to move his Cherry Hut to Martin's property on US 31. People in those days really worked hard to support each other—their relationships had very practical consequences.[39]

The youth of Benzie County and the surrounding area could always rely on a job picking cherries. The local papers often advertised the going rates that farmers were paying cherry pickers. As a result of the Great Depression, pay rates in 1931 were lower: cherry pickers would receive 1 ¼ cents per pound for sweet cherries, and twenty cents a lug of twenty-five pounds for sour cherries.[40] The following year saw rates drop even more, to ten cents a lug.[41] Despite the economic downturn, the cherries still needed to be picked; in 1936 the *Benzie Banner* advertised that there were jobs for 5,000 cherry pickers.[42]

In the early days at the new location in Beulah, the pies were baked in a stove heated with kerosene. Althea was nervous about lighting the stove, so she would go next door to the Sinclair Gas Station (now the Market Basket) to get a station attendant to come light the stove for her.

The amount and quality of cherries grown each year depended a great deal on Mother Nature. Pests such as fruit flies would appear occasionally.[43] Too much rain, a dry summer, an early freeze, or any other weather conditions could affect the size and quality of the local cherry crop, which also affected the prices that were set each year. Headlines such as "Estimates Half of Cherry Crop Killed by Frost," were common.[44]

One aspect of local business that was not affected by the Great Depression was the thriving resort business. In July 1936, the *Benzie Banner* reported that local resorts recorded four weekends in a row of "the largest crowd in years."[45] The following year, the headline was "Successful Benzie Resort Season Draws to a Close."[46] And in the *Bay City Times*, an article titled "Slump-Proof Resorts" began:

> *Traverse City, July 5—It's difficult to remember the depression when a big expensive car with an Illinois license drives up in front of a meat market and loads in $14.26 worth of meat and then hesitates in front of the fruit store, the grocery, the dry-cleaning establishment and the gasoline station before going back to the cottage.*[47]

For comparison's sake, a grocery store ad in the *Traverse City Record-Eagle* the month before advertised pork roast at 8 cents a pound, and frankfurters at 10 cents a pound.[48]

If anyone who's never been to northern Michigan wonders what the attraction is, this passage from a recent novel set in Suttons Bay says it best:

> *The majesty of Lake Michigan—stunning blues and greens—shimmered beyond the bay, which was tucked into a sandy corner of a lush green hillside, the thick boughs of towering pines waving at her. Cottages of all sizes dotted the hillside, windows making them resemble happy faces, long docks jutting out into the water. The orchards, colorful and symmetrical, sat atop the hill.*[49]

**Penn-Rad**
100% Pure Pennsylvania OIL
Unconditionally Guaranteed! The Finest
Motor Oil You Can Buy.
2 GAL. SEALED CONTAINER $1.00

| CERTO | Sure Jell | bottle 27c |
| LUCKY STRIKE CIGARETTES | | tin of 50 for 29c |
| LAUNDRY SOAP | White Eagle | 12 bars 25c |

**Scratch Feed** *Daily Egg Brand* 100-lb. bag $1.09

**Egg Mash** *Daily Egg Brand* 100-lb. bag $1.59

**Growing Mash** *Daily Egg Brand* 100-lb. bag $1.39

— IN A&P QUALITY MARKETS —

**Sliced Bacon** Cellophane Wrapped ½ Lb 9c

**Pure Lard** Refined 5 Lbs 25c

**Boiling Beef** Young and Tender. Per Lb. 8c

**Pork Roast** Per Lb. 8c

**Pork Steak** Per Lb. 10c

**Frankfurters or Bologna** Lb 10c

**Roasts** Of CHOICE BEEF Per Lb. 13c

**Boiled Ham** Wafer Sliced Per Lb. 29c

**A&P FOOD STORES**
The Great Atlantic & Pacific Tea Co.

A 1937 grocery ad reflects prices during the Great Depression.

Cherry tree blossoms promise delicious pies ahead.

**Claudia C. Breland**

## Celebrating Our Staff: 1930s

Jeanette Bailey

Margaret Case

Marjorie Case

Edith Chappel

Genevieve Chappel

Georgiana Knapp

Althea Kraker

Dorothy Kraker

J.L. Kraker

James Kraker Jr.

Claire Margaret Ley

Louise McGinnis

Addie Jane Rogers

Ella Smith

Margaret Stoops

Lucille Whitacre

# The 1940s

## Highlights of the Decade:

- **1942:** Althea Kraker managed The Cherry Hut while her brother Jim served in the Armed Forces during World War II
- **1942:** Cherry Festival in Traverse City cancelled until 1950 because of World War II
- **1946:** Jim Kraker returned to Beulah with his bride, Dottie, as new managers of The Cherry Hut

- **1946:** The jam kitchen opened in Benzonia; Althea Kraker married George Petritz
- **1946:** Leonard Case Jr. began working at The Cherry Hut jam kitchen
- **1947:** Althea and George Petritz developed their frozen pie business

**By 1940, the Great Depression was just about over,** and Althea and Jimmy Kraker had worked alongside their mother in The Cherry Hut for several years. That year, they were serving cherry pie, jellies and preserves, and light lunches. Althea remembers that as young children, whenever the ovens were lit they were banished with the admonition, "Out of the Hut! Out of the Hut!"[50]

In March of 1942, the first mention of sugar rationing was seen in the *Benzie Banner*, where it was announced that sugar rationing wouldn't start for another two weeks.[51] When the rationing did start, each household was required to list the names, hair and eye color, sex, and relationship to the head of the household, along with the exact amount of sugar in the home at the time.[52] Extra sugar was allowed for canning purposes.[53] Tart cherries require a lot of sugar, and at least one staffer recalls local grocers setting aside extra sugar for The Cherry Hut.[54] Althea Kraker remembers trying to cut back on sugar wherever they could, but "tart cherries take a lot of sugar!"

# Cherry Pie
## at the Cherry Hut

CHERRY PRODUCTS — LIGHT LUNCHES — CHERRY PIE

20th Season

## ALTHEA KRAKER

On U. S. 31 in Beulah next to Fay Hill's Sinclair Service

Ad in *Benzie Banner*

By April 1943, war bonds were being sold in Benzie County, with limited success.[55] Benzonia newspapers would publish regular notices as to how many rationing stamps were required for the allotted amount of sugar.[56] Eventually extra ration stamps were available for homemakers who did their own canning.[57]

Althea Kraker and friends pose in front of The Cherry Hut sign.

By July 1941, James "Jimmy" Kraker Jr. had received a non-resident tuition scholarship to study agricultural economics at Cornell University in Ithaca, New York.[58] This is where he registered for the draft.[59] He completed his training at the U.S. Navy Air Training Center in Pensacola, Florida, in 1943, where he married Dorothy Laidlaw Dodds.[60] After the war ended, Jimmy and Dottie returned to Benzie County; they managed The Cherry Hut until 1950, when they moved to New York.[61]

In the mid-1940s news of the war filled columns of the local newspapers. Notices of those killed, wounded, or missing in action made the front page.[62] To balance out the bad news, reports of those missing in action or prisoners in Germany having been released were also published.[63]

The year 1946 was a momentous one. Althea Kraker married George Karl Petritz in Frankfort, Michigan, on October 5, 1946.[64] George Petritz was a man with an extraordinary history; he served as an ensign in the Navy and commanded a patrol vessel in the Philippines, where he was captured in 1942 and spent more than two years as a prisoner of war.[65] He escaped from a Japanese prisoner ship after it was bombed, and swam to safety, being hidden by Filipino guerrillas until being rescued by Navy patrol boats.[66] George was awarded the Navy Cross and Purple Heart for acts of heroism.[67] After the war, Jimmy Kraker managed the restaurant and jam kitchen, while George and Althea Petritz began developing their frozen pie business.[68] In the first full year of operation of the Petritz Pie Company, they managed to make and sell 600,000 pies, each of them made in less than half a minute.[69]

## Gift Packages are Developed

In 1946, with the opening of the jam kitchen in Benzonia, the Krakers found an ever-increasing demand for their jams and jellies. They developed a cherry conserve containing sweet cherries and pecans—along with cherry jellies and preserves—to box up in a variety of ways for Christmas gifts.[70] One package contained a dozen jars of jelly: mint-flavored apple, strawberry, plum, grape, wild elderberry, currant, currant raspberry, apple, quince, crabapple, red raspberry, and of course, cherry. Jimmy Kraker told the *Benzie Banner* reporter that "distribution is nation-wide and that among his patrons are some famed celebrities, especially in the movie realm."[71] He also said that he was preparing a mailing of 10,000 advertising circulars.

Left: Cherry Hut gift packages offer an array of flavors.

Right: Which do you prefer?

Jimmy Kraker gets jams ready to ship.

Leonard Case Jr. began his career early, hired to work in The Cherry Hut jam kitchen at the age of fourteen. Leonard had deep roots in Benzie County; his great-grandfather Lucius Case had settled in the area by 1860 and his father (Leonard Case Sr.) was a justice of the peace.[72] Leonard would work at The Cherry Hut for the rest of his life, taking time away to get a business degree at Michigan State College and then serve two years in the army.[73] The Cherry Hut building on US 31 in Beulah was expanded, to help "adequately care for the overflow of tourist and local business that has literally swamped the place in recent years."[74] Additional staff were also hired.

Leonard Case works in the Benzonia jam kitchen.

Leonard Case stands next to stands of jam ready to ship out.

In the years after the war, Althea designed new uniforms for the girls. The red pinafores and white puffed-sleeve blouses, with black and white saddle shoes, would be the waitresses' standard look for more than a decade. Esther Rockwell was remembered for her many years of sewing The Cherry Hut uniforms.[75]

Phoebe Wolfe rolls pie crust by hand.

Rebecca Meek taking pies out of the oven.

These Cherry Hut beauties include (from left to right): Peggy Case, Marilyn Dressel, Judy Ewing and Mary Lonn Trapp.

Marcia Marshall (left) and Marilyn Hopkins are as pretty as the pies.

The deliciousness of Cherry Hut's cherry pie continued to spread beyond Michigan. The first cherry pie shipped by air was delivered to a lunch in Asbury Park, New Jersey.[76] And with the construction of a frozen pie facility on the north side of The Cherry Hut on US 31 in Beulah, customers all over the country could enjoy cherry pie.[77] The Pet-Ritz frozen pie plant was prominently featured in the *Benzie Banner* with a front-page photo of National Cherry Festival queen's attendant Marcia Ann Marshall, with a sixteen-inch cherry pie to be presented to President Truman.[78]

Even in the absence of the National Cherry Festival during the war years, one annual event that continued was the cherry pie baking competition in Benzie County. In 1947, the winner was eighteen-year-old Mrs. Dorothy (Schleuter) Reed, who had baked more than a thousand pies for The Cherry Hut the previous summer.[79] The following year Mrs. Althea Petritz of Beulah was one of the judges.[80]

And in 1948, a piece of cherry pie was still 20 cents.[81]

Customers line up for pie.

Jars, cans and fresh cherries for sale.

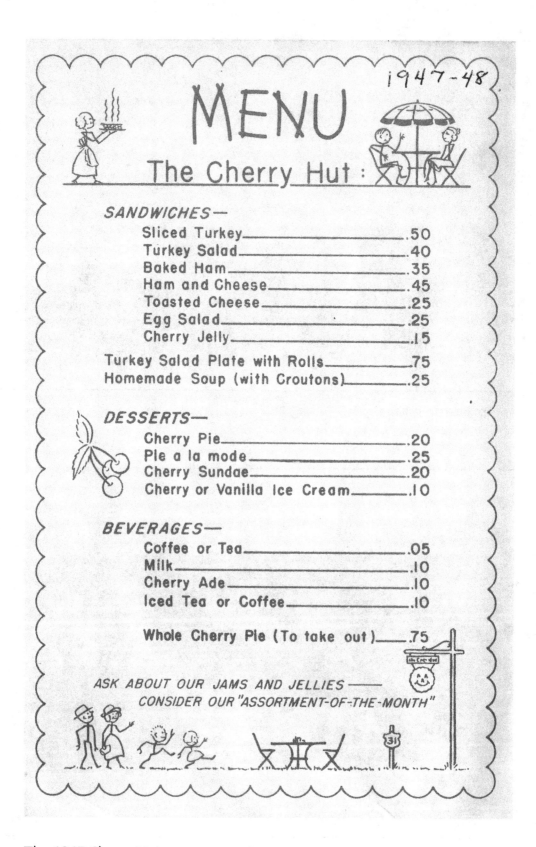

**MENU**
The Cherry Hut :

1947-48

SANDWICHES—
- Sliced Turkey ........................ .50
- Turkey Salad ........................ .40
- Baked Ham ........................... .35
- Ham and Cheese ...................... .45
- Toasted Cheese ...................... .25
- Egg Salad ........................... .25
- Cherry Jelly ........................ .15

Turkey Salad Plate with Rolls ........ .75
Homemade Soup (with Croutons) ........ .25

DESSERTS—
- Cherry Pie .......................... .20
- Pie a la mode ....................... .25
- Cherry Sundae ....................... .20
- Cherry or Vanilla Ice Cream ........ .10

BEVERAGES—
- Coffee or Tea ....................... .05
- Milk ................................ .10
- Cherry Ade .......................... .10
- Iced Tea or Coffee .................. .10

Whole Cherry Pie (To take out) ....... .75

ASK ABOUT OUR JAMS AND JELLIES——
CONSIDER OUR "ASSORTMENT-OF-THE-MONTH"

The 1947 Cherry Hut menu, page 1.

M-M-M SWEET!

– – –ANOTHER NEW-COMER to the

Cherry Hut Line is the finest

Pure Maple Syrup our northern sugar maples can

produce. And--after careful consideration, we

are introducing a new service we think you'll

like. We call it the ASSORTMENT-OF-THE-MONTH.

While you are here we suggest you look over our

wide variety of jams and jellies; select the

delivery plan you like best; then place your

order for future delivery. After you return from

your vacation, you will receive (monthly, or

bi-monthly) as you prefer, a variety assort-

ment selected for your family needs. All

winter long you will receive,

regularly, a well-balanced

assortment.

The Cherry Hut was Started in 1925

The 1947 Cherry Hut menu, page 2 with stick figures drawn by J.L. Kraker.

# ORDER BLANK

## CHERRY HUT PRODUCTS - JAMS AND JELLIES

### Beulah, Michigan

Please enter my order for the following:

| QUANTITY | ITEM | PRICE EACH | PER DOZEN | TOTAL |
|---|---|---|---|---|
| | *(In 16 Ounce Jars):* | | | |
| | Pure Cherry Preserves | 50¢ | $5.50 | |
| | Pure Cherry Jelly | 40¢ | 4.35 | |
| | Sweet Cherry Conserve | 55¢ | 6.00 | |
| | SPECIAL: 3-jar gift packages (One each of above) - $1.85 at the Cherry Hut- $2.25 when shipped. | | | |
| | *(In 12 Ounce Jars):* | | | |
| | Apple             Jelly | 30¢ | $3.25 | |
| | Crabapple              " | 30¢ | 3.25 | |
| | Red Currant            " | 35¢ | 3.80 | |
| | Currant-Raspberry      " | 40¢ | 4.35 | |
| | Wild Elderberry        " | 30¢ | 3.25 | |
| | Concord Grape          " | 30¢ | 3.25 | |
| | Guava                  " | 35¢ | 3.80 | |
| | Mint-Flavored Apple    " | 30¢ | 3.25 | |
| | Damson Plum            " | 35¢ | 3.80 | |
| | Quince                 " | 30¢ | 3.25 | |
| | Black Raspberry        " | 40¢ | 4.35 | |
| | Red Raspberry          " | 40¢ | 4.35 | |
| | Strawberry             " | 40¢ | 4.35 | |
| | ASSORTMENT-OF-THE-MONTH:   Six jars of assorted jellies and Jams - $3.25 shipped (prepaid) monthly◯ or bi-monthly◯ | | | |

For Shipments (except SPECIAL and ASSORTMENT-OF-THE-MONTH) add $1.00 per dozen (10¢ per jar in less than dozen lots). Minimum order shipped; 6 jars. 10% discount on any assorted dozen.

Enclosed please find: ( ) Check; ( ) Money Order in the amount of $

Name. . . . . . . . . . . . . . . . . . . . . . . . . . . . .

Address . . . . . . . . . . . . . . . . . . . . . . . . . . .

City. . . . . . . . . . . . . . .Zone . .State. . . . . . . .

( See reverse side for addressing of Gift Packages )

Cherry Hut menu, page 3, features jams and jellies available to order.

**From Pie Stand to Icon: The 100 Year History of *The Cherry Hut***

An introduction to our girls:

Marcia Ann Marshal, Beulah - Student at Ward Belmont

Mary Lonn Trapp, Beulah - Student at Benzonia High

Judy Ewing, Beulah - Also a Student at Benzonia High

Marcia Petitt of Benzonia - Student at U. of Michigan

Marilyn Dressel of Ann Arbor - Mich. State College.

Carolyn Hutchinson of Chicago - Montecello College.

Elizabeth Wolfe of Kanasa City - Park College, Mo.

Phoebe Wolfe of Kansas City - Student, Park College

Peggy Case of Benzonia - Student at Benzonia High.

Beth Lawliss of Benzonia - Student at Benzonia High.

Nancy Barrett of Flint - Student at Michigan State

We enjoy having you with us.

Come back again - real soon.

P. S.- We'd like to have you sign our Guest Book

Cherry Hut menu, page 4, begins an early tradition: naming the staff and their schools.

## Celebrating Our Staff: 1940s

Nancy Barrett

Peggy Case

Richard Clark

Marilyn Dressel

Marian Edwards

Kenny Ehman

Judy Ewing

Jane Garner

Mrs. Ralph Garner

Mary Heald

Carolyn Hutchinson

Althea Kraker

Dorothy Kraker

Dottie Kraker

J.L. Kraker

Jimmy Kraker

Beth Lawliss

Lee Logan

Marcia Ann Marshall

Becky Meek

Carolyn Osborn

Jay Pettit

Marcia Pettit

Dorothy Schleuter

Mary Lonn Trapp

Gordie Wallace

Elizabeth Wolfe

Jean Wolfe

Phoebe Wolfe

# The 1950s

## Highlights of the Decade:

- **1950:** Jim and Dottie Kraker moved to New York; J.L. Kraker took over the jam kitchen in Benzonia, and Althea and George ran The Cherry Hut.
- **1950:** The Petritz pie factory was relocated to the building north of The Cherry Hut, where people could watch pies being made. This was the first year frozen pies made at the factory were baked and sold at The Cherry Hut.
- **1950:** A profusion of cherries, too many for local pickers, resulted in the use of migrant workers in northern Michigan.
- **1951:** Mary Lonn Trapp was selected as National Cherry Queen.
- **1951:** A long jam counter was built to the north of The Cherry Hut to display and sell jams and other Cherry Hut products.
- **1955:** Pet-Ritz frozen pies was acquired by Pet Milk Co.
- **1955:** The Cherry Hut Scrapbook, now at the Benzie Area Historical Museum, put together by Barbara and Nancy Trapp.
- **1956:** Traverse City Cherry Hut closed.
- **1958:** Cherry Hut was advertised in the *New York Times*.
- **1958:** Dorothy Rogers Kraker passed away.
- **1959:** Leonard Case Jr. buys The Cherry Hut restaurant from George Petritz.

**After the lean war years,** the 1950s brought a general feeling of "happy days are here again." The decade started out with a bang with the news in February 1950 that Mr. and Mrs. James L. Kraker Jr. had sold Cherry Hut Products to George and Althea Petritz and were moving to New York state.[82] At this time George Petritz was exploring a new facet of the business: making and freezing cherry pies to be shipped all over the U.S.; the same year it was announced that his company had purchased the Benzie County Froz-n Foodbank.[83] Having this facility, which would continue its frozen locker rental service to area residents, would greatly increase the capacity of making and freezing cherry pies. George and Althea's business and family life in the village of Beulah was profiled in the May 1951 issue of *Redbook* magazine.[84]

A Pet-Ritz delivery driver proudly points to Beulah, a little town that gained national attention when Pet Milk bought Pet-Ritz in 1955.

By 1955, the national company Pet Milk got into the act by buying Pet-Ritz pie company and the Crystal Canning Company, both owned by George Petritz.[85] This news was publicized all the way to Hawaii, mentioning Beulah by name.[86] By 1959, Cherry Hut cherry pies joined a wide variety of other frozen pies marketed and sold by the Pet-Ritz company; part of their success was as a result of being advertised nationally on the *Red Skelton Show*.[87]

The cherry crop in the Grand Traverse region was always variable and depended on weather, insects, quality of the soil, and other factors. The years 1950 and 1951 were boom times for cherries, and it was impossible to hire enough local cherry pickers. As a result, for the first time, migrant workers from Mexico were flown in.[88] By the end of the season, over 15,000 migrant workers had been hired, causing a massive drop in population when they left.[89]

Up till now, the Cherry Growers Association usually met at the beginning of the season to discuss yields and agree on prices for their cherry harvest that year. But in 1950 that changed when a newspaper article stated that the price of cherries had not been set, and would be changing from day to day, sometimes falling to as little as 4 ½ cents per pound.[90] The following week, the Saint Joseph *Herald Press* carried a story about a Suttons Bay fruit farmer who gave his cherry pickers axes and ordered them to "destroy every tree in the orchard." (Which was about 250 of them.) The reason for the destruction was that he was offered only four cents a pound for his crop. "I'll clear the ground and raise strawberries," he declared.[91]

### Mary Lonn Trapp, Cherry Hut Staff and National Cherry Queen

Mary Lonn Trapp began working at The Cherry Hut in 1947 and became a manager in 1949.[92] Like many other staff members, she had deep roots in Benzie County as the granddaughter of pioneer Martin Trapp, on whose land The Cherry Hut stood.[93] On July 5, 1951, Mary Lonn (known as "Lonnie") made front page news around the state when she was chosen as the National Cherry Queen at Traverse City's annual National Cherry Festival.[94] Several articles were accompanied by photos of Lonnie relaxing at the beach, receiving her crown at the coronation ceremony, and appearing in various cities to promote Grand Traverse region cherries.[95] In September she completed a ten-day trip east to Washington, New York and Boston, promoting Michigan cherries and presenting state Senator Homer Ferguson with a cherry pie.[96] When Mary Lonn Trapp headed back to Michigan State College that fall, she was crowned Homecoming Queen.[97]

Mary Lonn Trapp, crowned the 1951 National Cherry Festival Queen, begins working at The Cherry Hut in 1947.

The Cherry Hut girls pose for a group photo.

When winter descends, so does business in the tourist towns of northern Michigan.

Ned Edwards was another staff member who worked at The Cherry Hut during the same time as Mary Lonn Trapp; he was famous—or infamous—for different reasons. As he tells it:

*I was hired at The Cherry Hut at age sixteen because of my parents' friendship with George and Althea Petritz. George hired me to do the dishwashing and pie baking; he explained that I'd be paid fifty cents an hour. I was to take the Montgomery Ward catalog and order my white dishwasher and cook's uniform, and the cost would be deducted from my pay at 30 cents an hour until paid for.*

*After reading the entire catalog, I ordered my uniform as well as a beautiful mahogany-stained ukulele with instruction book. When George got the bill he informed me that it would take over a month of my pay to cover, leaving me with almost no cash to buy food. So I started eating at The Cherry Hut, all the food I could find, which was free to employees. A glass or two of orange juice, a handful of roast turkey, a pie or two – who would miss it? But the disappearing food was noticed.*

*That was the first time I was fired. I was allowed to come back to work after promising not to eat any more food at The Cherry Hut without paying for it. Suddenly the policy was revised.*

*The ukulele proved to be very popular and was always available by the dishwasher to entertain the waitresses. I recall taking requests from the girls and learning the songs overnight. Customers would gather around the screen walls of the dishwashing room to hear the music until I was warned to cut down on the entertainment. But the girls loved it and encouraged me to keep singing, except when certain management was present.*

*In the early 1950s, the frozen pies were kept in the walk-in freezer in the building next door; in the cooler section were the hog carcasses. One of my jobs was to go over there twice a day to fetch pies, and I would always tag a waitress to come along & help me carry them. They cringed at the hogs, so we gave them names. One of them was "Uncle Joe."*

*The next incident happened one afternoon; it was raining hard and we had no customers because the dining area was still outside. Someone suggested we deal with our boredom by holding a funeral for Uncle Joe. With me leading the way, the whole staff processed next door to the cooler of the pie factory (now the auto parts store) carrying flowers picked from the Trapp Farm irrigation ditch behind the Hut. We sang "Poor Joe is Dead" with ukulele accompaniment, to the tune of "Poor Jud is Daid" from the hit musical 'Oklahoma.'*

Ned Edwards and his ukulele were popular with customers and fellow employees—but not always with the management.

**Claudia C. Breland**

*After I spoke the words of committal (I didn't know then I would become a Presbyterian minister) and sang an ode to Uncle Joe (which can be found in The Cherry Hut Scrapbook), we left the cooler. Standing in the yard between the pie factory and The Cherry Hut watching us recess with our flowers were Althea and George Petritz, the new owners. That was the second time I was fired; the next morning Althea yelled to me, "Ned, this job is just not working out for you!" I cried and promised not to do it again, and she let me stay on. I think it was because the ukulele still had to be paid for."*

After his stint at The Cherry Hut, Ned went on to meet his future wife Barbara "Bobbie" Trapp (also a staff member) at the end-of-season staff party in 1952. They married in 1956, and departed for Edinburgh, Scotland, where Ned entered the seminary.[98] In 1995 Ned and Bobbie Edwards began St. Andrew's Presbyterian Church in Beulah, where he was the pastor until he retired in 2002.[99]

### The Importance of Education

The town of Benzonia was founded with education in mind, with the development of Grand Traverse College—later renamed Benzonia Academy—being an integral part of the community from the start.[100] That focus on education continues to the present day, and is manifested in Cherry Hut's founders, owners, and staff. J.L. and Dorothy Kraker were both college graduates.[101] Cherry Hut staff were frequently named honor students in the local newspapers: Barbara Trapp and Margery Trapp made that list in 1953.[102] In 1955 Nancy Trapp was named Salutatorian of her graduating class at Benzonia High School.[103] The year before, Rita Rodriguez, another Cherry Hutter, was Salutatorian.[104] And in 1958 both Janet Case and her cousin Phyllis Case had their photos placed in the *Traverse City Record-Eagle* for being on the honor roll.[105]

Happy Hutters hitch a ride.

Featured on the front page of the *Benzie Banner*, 21 August 1952 was this little tidbit:

*HIGH STYLE—Beulah's famous "Cherry Hut Girls" get a big bang out of posing in this 1902 Cadillac when the owners stopped to sample a cherry pie last week. The car was one of thirty old-timers that recently made a tour of Michigan. Left to right are Mary Heald of Ann Arbor; Jeannie Drevdahl, Milan; Gordon Wallace, Ypsilanti; Mary Lonn Trapp, Beulah, and Lee Logan of Jackson. Gordon (the chauffeur) isn't really a "Cherry Hut Girl"—he's a chef.*

Throughout the decade, The Cherry Hut and the associated business Petritz Pies continued growing. In 1952 The Cherry Hut celebrated its 30th anniversary. It was around this time that the regular season was established: Cherry Hut would open on Memorial Day weekend and close on Labor Day. And on Saturday of Labor Day weekend, following the restaurant closing there would be a staff party.

The Cherry Hut celebrates its 30th anniversary!

With umbrellas all around, customers enjoy a summer day at The Cherry Hut.

Cherry Hut Daze — workers get ready to open for the season.

Effie serves up lunch for staff members.

**From Pie Stand to Icon: The 100 Year History of** *The Cherry Hut*

In 1950 a slice of cherry pie was 20 cents; on the 1959 menu it had gone up to 25 cents.

In March 1958, Cherry Hut hit another milestone when they placed an ad for their jams and jellies in the *New York Times*.[106]

May 3, 1958, saw the end of an era when Dorothy Rogers Kraker died in a hospital in Traverse City.[107] At the time of her death, she and her husband still had a part in The Cherry Hut business by operating The Cherry Hut Products gift store. In 1959, George Petritz sold The Cherry Hut restaurant to Leonard L. Case Jr., who had been manager there for several years.[108]

Never too young to help out: Althea Kraker Petritz and her daughter Chris.

Customers appreciate the shade on a sunny summer day.

With The Cherry Hut passing from the founders and creators of a "pie stand," having made and sold cherry treats and lunches during summer months under the Kraker family, to Leonard Case Jr., whose focus was to make it a full restaurant, many changes came about. The 1950s marked the end of the Hut operating only during the summer season and closing on Labor Day, always with a big celebration on the Saturday night of that weekend. It also marked the end of its staff being largely comprised of high school and college students (their schools always identified in the menus with their names) who experienced their summer jobs also as a social adventure, developing relationships and holding frequent parties at the homes and cottages of the staffers. For those who became a part of The Cherry Hut family, it

**"Our Three Products Posed For Your Pleasure"**

Our rigid requirements for superior quality are still the essence of our policy to produce only the best. We continue making Cherry Preserves from the finest fresh frozen red cherries available. This superior fruit and pure sugar, cooked to the right degree of perfection, compose this taste treat. Shimmering red Jelly with that smooth cherry tang, fills the jars marked "Pure Cherry Jelly." Filtered and pasteurized, the juice from the red cherry makes a jelly unexcelled in appetizing goodness. Our third cherry product in glass is our Sweet Cherry Conserve. This specialty product is made from the large black sweet cherries, and contains pecan nuts, oranges and lemons, in addition to the pure sugar we use in all our products.

**"12-Jar Gift Box — For Unmatched Appreciation"**

| | |
|---|---|
| 1 Doz. Jars Cherry Preserves | $6.50 |
| 1 Doz. Jars Cherry Jelly | 5.50 |
| 6 Jars Preserves, 6 Jars Jelly | 6.00 |
| 4 Jars Each—Preserves, Jelly, Conserve | 6.35 |

(Prices Include Express Charges)

This 12-jar gift box will be shipped, prepaid express, as a personal gift from you at the above prices. Especially packed in Yuletide finery (with your gift card), this dozen, or assorted dozen, jars will prove the ideal gift.

**"3-Jar Gift Package—The Ideal Remembrance"**

3-Jar Assorted Gift Package .................$2.10
(Prepaid Parcel Post)

One jar each of our Cherry Jelly, Cherry Preserves, and Sweet Cherry Conserve, make up this gift package. As pictured, the jars are packed in an attractive red cardboard box, with a cellophane window. Shredded red paper around the jars adds the final touch to this distinctive package. Your gift card will be included. For shipment this box is placed in a corrugated cardboard overwrap, and amply covered with holiday decoration.

Cherry Hut jams enjoyed as much popularity as the pies.

was almost like a summer camp experience in which you also had the bonus of getting paid. The camaraderie of the staff motivated them to gather before the Hut opened in the spring to make repairs, paint the building and signs, and begin their summer social adventure.

## Celebrating Our Staff: 1950s

Nancy Barrett

Jill Barrett

Mrs. Avery Bigelow

Barbara Brian

Marnie Calvird

Harold Case

Janet Case

Mary Lou Case

Peggy Case

Phyllis Case

Mary Ann Chamberlain

Bud Davis

Marilyn Dressel

Lois Drobena

Ned Edwards

Sally Ewing

Sandra Ewing

Sue Ewing

Patty Fleetwood

Mary Gaffney

Shari Greeley

Peggy Hall

Margo Hamilton

Jo Ann Heath

Delores Heinz

Katharine Hannewald

Virginia Hannewald

Carolyn Hutchinson

Andrea Johnson

Ann Johnson

Cynthia Kappus

Lee Logan

Bill Marshall

Dee Marshall

Kathryn McGee

Sandra Mead

Carol Miller

Dave Milliron

Suzanne Moore

Carol Neisman

Carolyn Ann Osborn

Nancy Payette

Karla Peterson

Kathleen Rankin

Rita Rodriguez

Virginia Rogers

Sandra Sherwin

Jean Taylor

John Taylor

Barbara Trapp

Marjorie Trapp

Nancy Trapp

Barbara Tyner

Jeanette Wallace

Nancy Wallace

Art Wolfe

Elizabeth Wolfe

Phoebe Wolfe

# The 1960s

**Highlights of the Decade:**

- **1960:** J.L. Kraker, founder of Cherry Hut, dies
- **1962:** Leonard Case elected president of Beulah-Benzonia Chamber of Commerce
- **1964:** Leonard Case constructs indoor eating area
- **1967:** Leonard Case buys Florida business Carolyn Candies
- **1969:** The Cherry Hut is up for sale—or is it?

**The year 1960 ushered in a new decade,** and with it, the winds of change. It also saw the departure of one of its founders when J.L. Kraker died in Frankfort on July 31, 1960.[109]

Leonard Case was an important member of the business community in Benzie County and donated both Cherry Hut products and a meeting place to community organizations. In 1961, Leonard hosted a Chamber of Commerce coffee break at The Cherry Hut, and the following year he was elected president of the Chamber.[110]

At Michigan State University, Cherry Hut products were showcased in an exhibit of new Michigan foods during a workshop for Ingham County club women. This workshop included a tour of Schmidt's supermarket in Okemos to view new products, including "tuna links and Chic-dogs" as well as banana flakes for making banana milkshakes and instant liquid coffee: one teaspoon added to boiling water, and your coffee is ready.[111] This indeed was the food of the future!

In 1964, Leonard Case made the decision to expand The Cherry Hut by adding an indoor dining area.[112] As a part of this upgrade, he placed a "For Sale" ad for a large Frigidaire ice maker, asking for $2400.[113] Always looking for new products to add, in 1967 he bought

Carolyn Candies in Orlando, Florida, planning on operating that business when he went south during the winter.[114] In 1969, Leonard obtained his pilot's license and then bought a small plane in order to make it easier for his commute south. When he was busy with The Cherry Hut in the summer, he would hire a manager to manage the candy business, which he owned until 1973.[115] Never content with the status quo, Leonard was always looking for ways to improve and innovate.

Leonard Case proudly stands in front of his Cessna 150.

The Cherry Hut was becoming more well-known across the state. A benefit card party hosted by St. Paul's guild of Business and Professional Women in Lansing featured table prizes of Cherry Hut jams and jellies.[116] A *Traverse City Record-Eagle* article on arts and crafts in Benzonia featured Muriel's Ceramics, Cherry Hut products, and Gwen Frostic's Presscraft Papers.[117] And if you're wondering why a jam and jelly producer would have been included in arts and crafts, a look at the article's author (Leonard L. Case Sr.) will answer that question. The Cherry Hut flexed its international reach when the Benzonia shop was featured on a tour of a women's group from Okinawa.[118]

By the late 1960s, The Cherry Hut's success had seen it grow from a single facility into a hodgepodge of wooden structures added on to the original building. In the back room, where the pies were put together and customers could watch the process through windows, staff would resort to putting sheets of cardboard in the windows to try to keep out the cold of brisk northern Michigan days.[119]

Sometimes online newspaper research, done decades after the event in question, will turn up interesting little mysteries for which there are no real answers. For instance, in 1969, for whatever reason, Leonard Case advertised The Cherry Hut for sale in the *Grand Rapids Press*.[120] The text of this "for sale" ad read:

RESTAURANT, The Cherry Hut—Beulah, Mich., fully equipped, 130 seating capacity, showing good profit in 10-week summer season operation with unlimited potential. Will be ready to open June 28. $22,500 down, by owner.

This ad ran only the one weekend, and only in the Grand Rapids newspaper; it did not appear in any Benzie County papers. Who knows what Leonard Case had in mind? Was he just testing the waters? Did any family members or friends dissuade him? We will probably never know.

In 1960 a piece of cherry pie was thirty cents; in 1969 it was forty cents.

A Cherry Hut postcard captures the fun of the 1960s.

Cherry Hut menu
1960

1960

# The Cherry Hut

**BEULAH, MICHIGAN**

*Now Serving Through Fall Color Tour Season*

## At the Counter is a full line-up of Cherry Hut Fruit Products and Gift Packages

**CHERRY PRODUCTS**

Sweet Cherry Conserve
Sweet Cherry Preserve
Cherry Preserves
Cherry Jelly
Cherry Jam
Cherry Sundae Sauce

Apple Jelly
Crabapple Jelly
Red Currant Jelly
Wild Elderberry Jelly
Concord Grape Jelly
Mint-Flavored Apple Jelly
Plum Jelly

**OTHER PURE FRUIT PRODUCTS**

Quince Jelly
Black Raspberry Jelly
Red Raspberry Jelly
Strawberry Jelly
Strawberry Preserve
Seedless Black
    Raspberry Preserve

Blackberry Jelly
Boysenberry Jelly

**CHERRY SYRUP**
**PURE MAPLE SYRUP**

## Cherry Jerry's HELPERS

**WRAPPED IT ALL BY MYSELF!**

To: A FRIEND

**THE GIRLS**

Kathy Kidder, Frankfort, Mich.
    Central Michigan University
Patricia Heffner, Beulah, Mich.
    Jackson Junior College
Mary Schaub, Joliet, Ill.
    University of Illinois
Kathleen Brown, Kalamazoo, Mich.
    Central Michigan University
Martha Smith, Coldwater, Mich.
    Coldwater High School
Barbara Hannewald, Benzonia, Mich.
    Benzie Central High School

Linda Hawkins, Dearborn, Mich.
    Central Michigan University
Carol Handren, Birmingham, Mich.
    Western Michigan University
Joyce Malott, Stanley, Wis.
    Manchester College
Cindy Bates, Milwaukee, Wis.
    Skidmore
Nancy Carlisle, Grosse Ile, Mich.
    Olivet College
Christine Gross, Hoffman Estates, Ill.
    Conant High School

**YOUR HOST**
Leonard Case, Jr., Proprietor

**HOSTESS**
Penny Eggleston, Binghamton, New York
Albany State University

**IN THE KITCHEN**
Mrs. Lois Drobena, Food Supervisor
Rita Carpenter, Breakfast Cook

**THE BOYS**

Don Brown, Kalamazoo, Mich.
    Loy Norrix High School
Lester Post, Crystal Lake, Ill.
    Central High School
James Meszaros, Beulah, Mich.
    Benzie Central High School

**THE BOYS**

Tom Haynes, Beulah, Mich.
    University of Michigan
David Van Hammen, Grand Rapids, Mich.
    Michigan State University
Steve Joy, Beulah, Mich.
    Graceland College

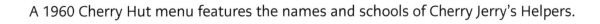

A 1960 Cherry Hut menu features the names and schools of Cherry Jerry's Helpers.

**Claudia C. Breland**

# The Cherry Hut

BEULAH, MICHIGAN

## BREAKFAST MENU

7:00 A.M. TO 11:30 A.M.

---

### Beulah Breakfast Bountiful

ORANGE OR TOMATO JUICE
TWO FRESH EGGS — HAM, BACON OR SAUSAGE
WAFFLES, PANCAKES OR FRENCH TOAST
POT OF COFFEE

**1.45**

---

**TWO FRESH EGGS COOKED IN BUTTER**
As You Like 'Em
With Ham . . . . . . . . . . . . . . . . 1.05
With Bacon . . . . . . . . . . . . . . . 1.05
With Sausage . . . . . . . . . . . . . 1.05
Above Served with Pot of Coffee and
Buttered Toast

**PANCAKES, WAFFLES OR FRENCH TOAST**
Featuring Pure Maple Syrup or Our Own
Cherry or Strawberry Syrup
With Ham . . . . . . . . . . . . . . . . 1.15
With Bacon . . . . . . . . . . . . . . . 1.15
With Sausage . . . . . . . . . . . . . 1.15
Above Served with Pot of Coffee

### Side Orders

Orange or Tomato Juice . . . . . . . . . . . .20
One Egg and Toast . . . . . . . . . . . . . . .40
Two Eggs and Toast . . . . . . . . . . . . . .60
Bacon, Sausage or Ham . . . . . . . . . . .40

Waffles, Pancakes or French Toast . . . . .60
Cinnamon Roll . . . . . . . . . . . . . . . . .15
Toast . . . . . . . . . . . . . . . . . . . . . . .15
Pot of Coffee . . . . . . . . . . . . . . . . . .15

Cereal . . . . . . . . . . . . . . .25, with Half & Half .35

For Breakfast Toppings we Feature Local Pure Maple Syrup or Cherry and Blueberry Topping Made in Our Own Jam Kitchen. These Pure Syrups may be Purchased at Our Jam Counter.

WHOLE CHERRY HUT CHERRY PIE TO TAKE OUT 96c

HOURS
BREAKFAST
7 A.M. — 11:30 A.M.
FULL MENU
10 A.M. — 9 P.M.
BEVERAGES AND DESSERTS ONLY
9 P.M. — 10 P.M.

The Cherry Hut serves up a "Beulah breakfast bountiful" for just $1.45.

## Celebrating Our Staff: **1960s**

Julie Augustine

Betsy Barnett

Cindy Bates

Anna Bennett

Andrea Black

Janice Bowling

Dave Brown

Don Brown

Kathleen Brown

Joseph Campbell

Rita Carpenter

Nancy Carlisle

Mike Cox

Tom Crain

Norm Deering

Mary Jane Derby

Lois Drobena

Penny Eggleston

Carol Ellison

Ellen Engelhart

Debby Fisher

Dorothy Foltz

Herb Foresman

Rowland Gehring

Cynthia Gilroy

Priscilla Gilroy

Charlie Gregory

Christine Gross

Carol Handren

Barbara Hannewald

Marsha Hanson

Carolyn Harris

Dianna Hawkins

Linda Hawkins

Sally Hayden

Tom Haynes

Patricia Heffner

Kathe Hikade

Sue Hobart

Mike Horton

Jane Johnson

Steve Joy

Paul Kappus

Sonja Keiller

Kathy Kidder

Sue Kirkpatrick

Linda Kronlund

Marian Kujawa

Becky La Salle

Beulah Loewen

Bonnie Logan

Margo Luyendyke

Joyce Malott

Pat Mead

James Meszaros

Andrew Miller

Bob Morris

John Murphy

Bill Neale

Peggy Orr

Betsie Peckham

Dorothy Petritz

Chris Petritz

Don Post

Lester Post

Susan Prange

Sue Rittschof

Sally Robotham

Sally Rogers

Judy Romsek

Kitty Rosa

Mary Schaub

Martha Smith

Bill Spencer

Patsy Stiles

Midge Stone

Jan Swander

David Van Hammen

Cathy Veldhuis

Libby Veldhuis

Terry Witt

Helen Wolfe

MaryEllen Wolfe

Connie Wood

# The 1970s

**Highlights of the Decade:**

- **1970:** Rick Van Hammen begins working as a dishwasher & pie baker
- **1971:** Cherry Hut expands their dining area; last vestiges of original Cherry Hut removed to make room for a modern food kitchen

- **1972:** Leonard Case Jr. marries Brenda Joy Deering
- **1972:** Cherry Hut celebrates its 50th anniversary
- **1977:** Food writers Jane and Michael Stern visit The Cherry Hut for the first (but not the last) time

**In 1970, fifteen-year-old Rick Van Hammen,** following his older brothers' examples, presented himself at The Cherry Hut to apply for a job. Rick recalls, "At that point there was no application form, just Leonard and his legal pad. Although he generally didn't hire anyone younger than sixteen, he said he'd take a chance on me."[121] Rick was initially hired to wash dishes and bake pies; later he was promoted to kitchen duty. At the end of 2021 he had completed his 50th year of working at The Cherry Hut, most of those years spent as the kitchen manager. As a mark of respect to Rick and his legacy, he is noted on the menu as "The Iron Man."

In 1972 Leonard took on a life partner when he married Brenda Joy Deering.[122] A speech therapist for schools in Utica, Michigan, she and Leonard were married at Benzonia Congregational Church on June 24, 1972.[123] Brenda began working alongside Leonard, and when their children Andrew and Amanda were old enough to do simple chores, they joined in.

Our "Iron Man" Rick Van Hammen.

Rick Van Hammen prepping the Cherry Hut for its 100th season and his 51st season!

The staff and management of The Cherry Hut always found a way to participate in community activities. A good example is the National Coho Salmon Festival that took place in Honor, Michigan, in June 1972. The Cherry Hut was listed as a sponsor, along with many other well-known businesses such as Case Motors, the Pine Not Resort, and the Beulah Thriftway.[124]

In January 1972, the news hit the papers that the Benzie County Co-Operative was filing for bankruptcy.[125] Future staffer Warren Call's great grandfather Chauncy J. Call was active in the co-op as far back as 1959.[126] The co-operative had formed in 1922 to support farmers and orchardists, maintaining a building-supplies business there in the county.

In October 1977, the Sleeping Bear Sand Dunes were officially dedicated as a National Park.[127] This created an additional attraction to draw visitors to the area. However, this came with a downside as well: in the mid-seventies the Traverse City Cherry Festival was drawing thousands of tourists. This was a boon for the merchants and restaurants, but created more work for law enforcement, public health, trash disposal and traffic control.[128]

Food writers Jane and Michael Stern visited The Cherry Hut for the first time in 1977. For the next thirty years they would write about The Cherry Hut in *Gourmet, Bon Appetit*, and in their books *Roadfood* and *Goodfood*. Other food writers from local and national magazines and newspapers, reading their reviews, soon found their way to The Cherry Hut.

Although Leonard Case was always looking to improve his products and services, the staff members were a little more conservative. At least one former staff member remembers that any whiff of change was met with some doubt; for example, the fear that indoor dining would change the character of the restaurant. ("Hamburgers on the menu? It's all downhill from here!")[129]

And an ad for The Cherry Hut in the *Benzie County Record Patriot* in September 1979 showed just how far the restaurant had come since its beginnings:

**THE CHERRY HUT RESTAURANT**

U.S. 31
BEULAH
882-4431

Continental Breakfast
Lunch · Dinner

SELECTION OF THE DAY

| | |
|---|---|
| SUNDAY | BAKED CHICKEN |
| MONDAY | (Mushroom Gravy) MEAT LOAF |
| TUESDAY | SWISS STEAK |
| WEDNESDAY | ROAST PORK |
| THURSDAY | ROAST BEEF |
| FRIDAY | SEAFOOD |
| SATURDAY | BAKED STUFFED PORK CHOP |

Enjoy air conditioned dining in our new expansion.
Dinners include choice of beverage and dessert.

New fall hours: 11 a.m. to 8 p.m. daily
Closed on Tuesday

This ad for The Cherry Hut promotes a new feature—air conditioning!

The Cherry Hut now had air conditioning, and was open from 11 a.m. to 8 p.m., serving Continental Breakfast, Lunch and Dinner.[130]

Margo Waring was hired as a baker in 1973 and worked for eight years or more in The Cherry Hut kitchen. She walked over at 6 a.m. and baked cherry pies and cinnamon rolls alongside her good friend Beulah Loewen, earning $3.25 an hour. One of her favorite things was talking to the people who were outside the kitchen window, watching the pies being made. One day, after overhearing another younger worker asking for a raise, Margo decided that she wanted to have a raise, too. She got up the courage to talk to her neighbor and Cherry Hut owner, Leonard Case. When Leonard asked why she needed more money, Margo said, "For self-esteem." Margo got the raise![131]

Cinnamon rolls, fresh from the oven!

Neil Marshall was hired during the 1970s and rose to eventually become Assistant Manager. He remembers:

*One of my favorite Cherry Hut traditions is the inclusion of the schools attended by the employees listed on the back of the menu. And it's not just window dressing. Many young people from Benzie County and the upper Midwest have used summers at The Cherry Hut to help pay for their education. My co-workers at the restaurant went on to become doctors, dentists, optometrists, nurses, social workers, attorneys, engineers, and teachers. I learned early on that education was valued at The Cherry Hut. When I rode up on my bright yellow Schwinn Manta Ray to apply for my first job at age fifteen, the interview was limited in scope. Leonard asked how I did in* school and when I replied, "O.K.," he straightened a bit and pinned me with a piercing stare. "Honor Roll?" When I replied in the affirmative, he suddenly barraged me with a series of mental arithmetic problems. I nervously lobbed answers back and the interview was over. When I reported for duty the next day, he handed me an old push broom and shovel and told me to clear the winter-time accumulation of dirt, gravel, leaves, and trash from the parking lot and driveway. It took hours. As I was sweeping, I concluded that perhaps I hadn't done as well with my mental arithmetic test as I thought I had.

Another wonderful trait of The Cherry Hut is its remarkable degree of staff retention. This works as a nice counterbalance to the annual loss of those who finish their schooling and launch upon their professional careers. Season after season, the "old hands" return for another go. A case in point: the young man who taught me to wash dishes and bake pies in 1975 has continued to answer the siren call of The Cherry Hut every year since then and now serves as kitchen manager. This sort of thing doesn't happen by accident. The Case family has done a fantastic job of fostering a wholesome environment where young people, some just entering the workforce, can meld into the bustling operation of a sizable restaurant. The work can be challenging and fast-paced, but the upbeat, "we're-all-in-this-together" team attitude keeps it fun and rewarding. The Cherry Hut is a family restaurant in the very best sense.

Leonard was a disciplined record-keeper. He also enjoyed a good dip in Crystal Lake on a beautiful summer day. Occasionally these two impulses conflicted. One hot August afternoon, a customer approached the young lady manning the cash register and angrily demanded to speak to the manager. "Of course," the cashier replied. "Can I inform him what the problem is?"

"There is a man sitting at a table on the patio wearing a wet bathing suit and a bathrobe!" the customer fumed.

The cashier leaned forward to glance out the door toward the patio. "Oh, that IS the manager, Ma'am." Leonard had apparently interrupted his swim to log his three o'clock sales records.

Ney Hawkins, who I knew had been a grade-school classmate of my grandparents—meaning he was no spring chicken—served The Cherry Hut for years as handyman extraordinaire. He fixed things, painted, did some general maintenance, and helped make jam. His sardonic sense of humor was always on full display. "I need someone with a strong back and a weak mind," he'd often say when needing assistance with something, "and you'll do just fine." He returned from a cross-country trip unimpressed with pretty much everything he'd seen, including the Grand Canyon: "Make a mighty fine landfill, if you ask me." So, I was totally unprepared the day we were *driving back from the jam kitchen and Ney suddenly pulled over and stopped on the shoulder of the road. He gestured past me out the window and commanded, "Look at that." He had parked next to a huge rose bush, covered in blossoms. "How can anyone see that and then say there is no God?" We idled there for a few moments, staring in reverential silence at the roses, then without another word Ney dropped the truck back into gear and we continued on our way. I learned an important lesson about judging other people that day.*

Leonard and Brenda Case with son Andy.

Chris Petritz McInnes recalls working at The Cherry Hut in 1965 and 1966, "but I almost didn't get the job because I failed Leonard's mental arithmetic test! I still can't do math in my head!"

This decade started out with a piece of cherry pie being priced at forty cents and ended in 1979 at double the price.

Long-time staff member Kay Holt remembers:

*The Cherry Hut has been a part of my life essentially forever. As a child, it was the place to go for a super special treat with Grandma. As a teenager, it was my first* job, as an adult it was my first true experience in total responsibility, and it is still an integral part of my "mature" life today. I cannot imagine what my life would be without the memories, the friendships, and the life experiences I have from belonging to the "Hut Family."

In 1973, I became part of the Hut when my parents informed me that if I wanted certain things, I needed to find a way to pay for them. It was summer at the cottage—yes, I was and still am a fudgie—so my thoughts turned to waitressing at The Cherry Hut. After a fairly intense interview first with Leonard and then with Brenda, I knew I had found my niche. High school days with high school pay, but also fabulous benefits—ranging from delicious food on breaks, to great tips, to fun co-workers, and most importantly friendship with two of the nicest people I have ever known which has grown to include their son Andy, his wife Christy, and their boys, Carson and Caleb.

How can I forget being in my late teens and enjoying summer evenings at the Outlet and Mary G. getting poison ivy (again and again) or going to Van Hammen's bunkhouse? The fun and camaraderie never ended; even though we might wish that the busboys would stop dropping ice cubes in our change pockets—which of course we didn't notice, until it was dripping down our legs! It was hard work and many's the night I went home and walked straight into the lake, clothes and all, just to cool off. It sure was fabulous when the "new" addition was added, and we had many more tables in the blessedly cool air of a second dining room. Funny, thing: it was built around 40 years ago, and we still call it the "new" not to be confused with the "super new" addition of 2004. I guess when you're 100 years old, "new" is a relative term!

It was in the early '80s that Leonard and Brenda asked me to run the restaurant so they could do a family reunion weekend which evolved into a week here, a weekend there while they and Andy and Amanda took some well-deserved family vacations. Those were the times I truly realized what an amazing place The Cherry Hut was. It was hard work, and dedication, and long, long hours put into making The Hut a place people would enjoy and would want to come back to for another visit. I loved getting to be a part of that side of the restaurant.

I could go on and on with memories of the Hut: the year Leonard had his first heart attack and Brenda and I went crazy trying to keep him away from the restaurant; trying to prove we could run the business without him—AS IF— and he knew it, so when he would sneak over, we pretended we didn't see him for about 15 minutes, then we chased him back home. Or the year my son, Phillip, came to work and would tell stories of making jam. Or being asked to be one of the Managers—a true highlight of my life.

My "real" job is teaching, but my summer fun has been and continues to be working at The Cherry Hut. I am retiring this year from school, but I don't know if I can ever retire from The Cherry Hut. How can I go all summer without seeing the regulars come in and catching up on all that's happened over the winter? Or having people come in with their children and now their children's children to continue their own family tradition? Or being surprised at seeing one of my students from Sylvania pop in with their family because they have heard me talk about "my" restaurant? For now, anyway, I can't.

I cannot thank Leonard and Brenda enough for welcoming me into their family business back in 1973. I will never forget who I was when I started here and who I have grown to be as a result of knowing them and of course now Andy and Christy who continue to carry on the Case legacy with pride, seeing their work ethic, and being around the people who come to The Cherry Hut: the locals, the summer people, and the co-workers coming together for the wonderful experience that is The Cherry Hut. Thank you to everyone for being such an important part of my life.

Congratulations to The Cherry Hut on its 100-year birthday! Here's to the next 100! May you continue to bring joy to everyone who plays a part in this Northern American Tradition! To borrow a phrase: "Cherry on!"

## Celebrating Our Staff: 1970s

| | | | |
|---|---|---|---|
| Julie Augustine | Len Burns | Leslie Dennis | Herb Foresman |
| Mark Bair | Lorri Burns | Dede Dieckman | Sue Froelich |
| Toni Barber | Chris Byers | Elizabeth Doane | Janet Fuksa |
| Anna Bennett | Ruth Cartlidge | Kay Drexel | Sarah Gibson |
| Marcia Bourdo | Philip Catton | Cindy Drobena | Denise Goodreau |
| Cheryl Bouschor | Becky Clark | Lois Drobena | Charlie Gregory |
| Sue Bradley | Mike Clark | Edna DuBois | Christine Gross |
| Dan Brown | Diane Coles | Shelley Egan | Mary Gross |
| Dave Brown | Pamela Cook | Rachel Evans | |
| Don Burns | Tom Crain | Connie Evey | **CONTINUED ON NEXT PAGE** |
| Eric Burns | Debbie Crawford | Ann Fitch | |

Lynnette Hammond

Marsha Hanson

Carolyn Harris

Ney Hawkins

Angela Hendricks

Chris Hitchcock

Liz Hitchcock

Kay Holt

Nancy Hopkins

Peter Hopkins

George Horn

Mike Horton

Cheryl Jessop

Jane Johnson

Tim Johnson

Sarah Johnson

Jane Kamp

Shelly Kaphammer

Charlene Katz

Kris Kime

Cherie Klomparens

Kathy Klomparens

Marian Kujawa

Susan Kyser

Terri Lalas

Jeanne Lauth

Lynette Letcher

Jim Letcher

Beulah Loewen

Lynn Loney

Sarah Lutes

Margo Luyendyke

Laura Marshall

Neil Marshall

Robert Marshall

Debbie Michael

Kelly Milliron

Blake Milliron

Andrew Miner

Ann C. Morrow

John Murphy

Laurie Murphy

Tom Northway

Kelley Oliver

Laura Payment

Andrew Peters

Lynn Pettit

Dorothy (Dosie) Petritz

Mimi Petritz

Don Post

Nancy Preston

Laurie Raymond

Maria Ream

Nancy Rich

Sally Robotham

Lisa Rogers

Sally Rogers

Kitty Rosa

Theresa Sanchez

Donna Santer

Ed Scarbrough

David Scott

Evelyn Scott

Julie Scott

Steve Scott

Beth Sheets

Nancy Smith

Steve Stahl

Patsy Stiles

Kay Thompson

Michelle Thompson

Jane Tidey

Debbie Torpe

Dave Van Hammen

Phil Van Hammen

Rick Van Hammen

Tom Van Hammen

Mary Van Pelt

Jim Veldhuis

Leslie Wanner

Clair Waterson

Jerri Waterson

Carolyn White

Sabine Wicher

Beth Wing

Chris Wolfe

David Wolfe

Linda Wolfe

Wendy Wolfe

Connie Wood

# *The 1980s*

**Highlights of the Decade:**

- **1980:** Northern dining room, patio and modern bakery added
- **1983:** Jane and Michael Stern publish a new book called *Goodfood*
- **1986:** Remodeling completed

**After at least two editions of *Roadfood*** (Cherry Hut being listed in both), Jane and Michael Stern published *Goodfood: The adventurous eater's guide to restaurants serving America's best regional specialties.*[132] Possibly the first magazine where the Sterns mentioned

Leonard Case Jr. in his office.

The Cherry Hut was *People* magazine in 1983, where they said, "The squinty grin of mascot Cherry Jerry was first carved into The Cherry Hut pie crust in 1922."[133]

Cherry Hut began to be mentioned regularly in midwestern newspapers. Titles such as "Michigan's Amazing Autumn," "Cherry Pie-Pickin' Time," and "Jerry a Cherry Hut fixture," profiled the restaurant in glowing terms.[134] That last article, in the *Benzie County Record Patriot*, featured two photos by Cherry Hut staffer Tom Northway: one of The Cherry Hut in the 1940s with open-air dining, and the other a family photo of Leonard and Brenda Case with their children, Andy and Amanda.

Long-time staff member Melissa Burch Nelson writes:

*It was the Summer of 1986; the end of my junior year in high school. I started waitressing at The Cherry Hut for Leonard and Brenda. It was my first "real" job. I always said that working for the Cases taught me how to be a good employee. They had high expectations, and as a 16-year-old, I didn't want to disappoint them. Leonard was a man of few words, but when he would ask a question about school, family, or your life, you knew that he did care about you. Brenda spent a lot of time at the restaurant and was always there to ensure that the customers received the best from all the wait staff.*

*I continued to waitress in the summers for the next eight years. During those years, I had the best summers meeting waitresses from all over. Many of the girls had cottages on the lake and had a "Summer Job" at The Cherry Hut. I made lifetime friends from my summers there. We would work our shifts, then hang out at night at Cherry Hut bonfires. The best part was that we had as much fun working together as we did hanging out in the evenings. We eventually graduated from college, started our careers and moved on from The Cherry Hut. Those summers truly were the best.*

*My younger brother, Bill, also spent many years working at The Cherry Hut. He spent the summers washing dishes, taking out the trash, cleaning the bathrooms, baking the pies and forming lifetime friendships, as well.*

*Summer of 2007, after 14 years of being away from Michigan, my husband, three daughters, and I moved back home after my husband retired from the Marine Corps. We wanted to raise our daughters in Benzie County. While I was applying for teaching positions, I decided that I'd see if Leonard needed any waitresses for the summer. At this point, Andy Case was managing the restaurant and he said he could use some help. I did it! I put that uniform back on as a middle-aged woman!*

*I love working at The Cherry Hut so much that I continue to work my summers there, to this day. As a teacher, I have my summers off and it just works. The best part is that all three of my daughters have/or still do waitress with me. Riley worked there for nine years, this summer will be eight years for Morgan and Peyton has worked there for seven years. One of those lifetime friends I referred to previously, is a teacher and she came back too. I grew up working at The Cherry Hut and it is an honor to share my love of this business and the Case family!*

A typical tour group was the Park Forest Singers from Tinley Park, Illinois, who spent part of August 1989 at the Interlochen Music Camp. In between rehearsals for a performance of Mendelssohn's *Elijah*, they made field trips to Beulah and Benzonia, visiting The Cherry Hut and Gwen Frostic's Presscraft Papers.[135] An article in an August 1987 issue of the *Benzie County Record Patriot* said, "Cherry Jerry has had both eyes on The Cherry Hut for 65 years—one on the past and one on the present."[136]

By the mid-1980s The Cherry Hut was truly a family-run business. Andy remembers dusting the jam shelves and putting away clean dishes. In an interview, his mother, Brenda remembers that his first chore was picking up paper and trash in the parking lot; as she put it, "He learned the business from the ground up."[137] As he grew older, Andy would start helping with the jam production.

The staff at Cherry Hut were always looking to develop new products. Their selection of jams and jellies had greatly expanded over the years, and one popular item from the earliest days was cherry conserve.[138] Another item that started being mass produced and available for sale at The Cherry Hut in the mid-1980s was locally developed and produced dried cherries.[139]

Beulah Loewen takes a bakery break.

**Claudia C. Breland**

Amanda Case with her grandmother June Deering in The Cherry Hut kitchen.

Former Cherry Hut staffer Angela Knauer wrote in her book, *With a Cherry on Top:*

*My first job ever was at The Cherry Hut. It was a challenge to find the required black and white saddle shoe oxfords (Golden Shoes on Front Street in Traverse City was the only place that carried them), and to pedal my bike to work every day the summer of my fifteenth year. But it was fun. The girls I worked with became my friends, and we still maintain contact after more than twenty years. I returned there to work other summers, referring to my bright red pinafore dress and crisp white blouse as my "costume." I was drawn back because there was a sense of family, and the customers who returned every summer and watched us grow into adulthood were always wonderful.*

*Leonard Case (Andrew's dad) has kept all of the old menus with the names of servers and bakers printed on the back for posterity. A former dishwasher and pie-baker is now a well-respected local optometrist. One of my good friends from that first summer now works for FEMA and the Secret Service. Another has been a teacher in battle-torn Iraq. Some have gone on to greater fame: I believe Mary Gross from Saturday Night Live worked there as a kid."*[140]

*The saddle shoes we wore became a thing of the past in the mid to later 1980s when my friend Carla Gipson was talking with Rachelle Johnson who was a cheerleader at Benzie Central. She had saddle oxford athletic shoes that were far more comfortable than the standard models we'd been wearing for years. Carla, our head waitress at the time, had Brenda Case's ear and showed them to her from the JC Penney catalog. Brenda thought they looked really nice and allowed us to wear them in red & white or black & white. This was a vast improvement for us girls as we put in a lot of steps every day during our shifts! Now the staff can wear more varied footwear, focused on comfort while keeping the traditions of quality service and great food!*

*Also, when I was working as office manager at Triple D. Orchards, Inc. in Empire, Andy leased some warehouse space for product from us. When Leonard would come up to pick up product it was great because he would come and hang out for a bit with me in my office. It was an honor that the Big L made a point to come see me at those times. He was one of the best bosses I ever had.*

Leonard Case Jr. with Brenda Case, Andy and Amanda.

Long-time staff member Missy Goold writes,

*I started working for the Case family in 1984. I was 17 years old and it was my first real job. I was really scared of Leonard and a little bit scared of Brenda. But it turns out they were great bosses. The whole Case family have been great bosses. I have watched Andy grow up and I now have the privilege of watching his two sons grow up. I have worked with some great people that I am proud to call my friends. We are all part of The Cherry Hut family.*

**Claudia C. Breland**

*I have learned a lot in the many years I have worked for The Cherry Hut. I have learned from veteran coworkers, from new coworkers and from customers. I have learned to cook, clean to code and put out a product that keeps people coming back. But I think the most important lesson that I learned was about success. To be successful and be so year after year, you have to trust those you work with and also be trustworthy and reliable for them and the customers. To do what needs to be done, even when it seems impossible. When you work with and for people like that day after day it binds you together. It makes you a family.*

*I once heard a customer ask Andy if he was Cherry Jerry. Andy responded that we are all a little bit of Cherry Jerry.*

*It doesn't surprise me that The Cherry Hut is still in business after 100 years. I have seen it from the inside and the outside and it is an amazing sight to behold. I am so grateful of the wonderful gift that was given to me by Cherry Jerry and the Case family. Thank you! Here's to another 100 years!!!*

A 1985 Cherry Hut ad congratulates its graduates.

In 1982 a piece of cherry pie is $.95; by 1989 it rises to $1.35.

## Celebrating Our Staff: 1980s

Nancy Acklin

Deanna Alsup

Cathy Armstrong

Jeff Bair

Leslie Bair

Mark Bair

Mike Bair

Pam Bair

Steve Bair

Kathy Bissell

Dave Bowers

Katie Bowers

Rolly Brown

Kimberly Bull

Don Burns

Eric Burns

Jim Burns

Patty Callam

Deb Canfield

Amanda Case

Andrew Case

Bill Case

Brenda Case

Leonard Case

Lynn Case

Craig Caugh

Tammy Clink

Sandra Cook

Jolene Crooks

Chauna Cumpian

Sandra Dant

Kitty Darnell

June Deering

Ken Dilas

Ronda Dobson

Edna DuBois

Virginia Dunlop

Laurie Erdman

Michelle Erdman

Susan Erskine

Rachel Evans

Rebecca French

Maxine Gatrell

Carla Gipson

Lisa Girven

Missy Goold

Lynette Hammond

Dorothy Hawkins

Jerry Hawkins

Kim Hawkins

Ney Hawkins

Amanda Helferick

Minda Helferick

Paul Hoffmeyer

Jeannine Hough

Jennifer Hough

Sara Hough

Lori Inman

Rachelle Johnson

Christopher Joy

Donald Joy

Carol Kelly

Daniel Kinske

Kathleen Kinske

Angela Knauer

Loraine Laguire

Terri Lalas

Sharon Lean

Elizabeth Lee

Sheila Leers

Brenda Lewis

Beulah Loewen

John Lopez

Michelle Lopez

Sharon Lopez

Teresa Loranger

Scott Loree

Marianne Maddock

Connie Marshall

David Marshall

Donna Marshall

John Marshall

Jenny Marshall

Julie Marshall

Laura Marshall

Neil Marshall

CONTINUED ON NEXT PAGE

## Celebrating Our Staff: 1980s (continued)

Tim Mauntler

Melissa McArthur

Mitzi McKay

Mike McPherson

Jennifer Milliron

Kelly Milliron

Mishelle Miller

Paul Murphy

Melissa Nelson

Susan Northway

Diane Priest

Steven Parks

Mary Jo Robotham

Jacki Rodriguez

Mary Rodriguez

Alan Rose

Kimberly Sanchez

Ed Scarbrough

Sandra Scarbrough

Carolyn Scott

Helen Scott

Julie Scott

Steve Scott

Elisa Shultz

Hope Smeltzer

Anne Smith

Sarah Snyder

Steve Souders

Susan Soule

Shannon Sproul

Karen Swisher

Mark Tolosa

Deborah Torp

Carla Van Farowe

Rick Van Hammen

Craig Ware

Margo Waring

Margaret Wildie

Josh Williams

Christopher "Topher" Wolfe

Kelly Yenger

# The 1990s

**Highlights of the Decade:**

- **1992:** Cherry Hut celebrates its 70th anniversary
- **1992:** Cherry Hut featured in the *Wall Street Journal*
- **1999:** Andrew Case graduates from Michigan State University with a degree in Restaurant Management
- **1999:** Cherry Hut mentioned in *USA Today*: "10 great places to eat pie"

**By 1990, The Cherry Hut was offering more dining choices** to their customers than ever before. During the summer season they were open from 11 a.m. to 9 p.m., with a breakfast buffet on the weekends. Customers could enjoy a soup & sandwich for $3.15, or a complete dinner for as little as $6.50.[141]

On June 13, 1992, The Cherry Hut celebrated its 70th anniversary by featuring a replica of the 1959 menu.[142]

Also in 1992, The Cherry Hut was featured in an article in the *Wall Street Journal*, titled "Old Fashioned Frugality is Back in Fashion," stating that "these companies are generally less enamored of name-brand prestige and more concerned with good value." The Cherry Hut's package of three 16-ounce jars of Montmorency Cherry Sundae Sauce for $11.75 including shipping was cited as an example.[143]

In 1993, fourteen-year-old Warren Call was hired to wash dishes and bake pies. He remembers at his interview (no application, just Leonard and his legal pad) Leonard asking him, "Are you any relation to Royal Call?" When Warren said that Royal was his grandfather, Leonard said, "You're hired!" Warren rose in the ranks to become assistant manager—supervising the cashiers, busboys and wait staff, along with pitching in wherever he was needed.

**THE CHERRY HUT
RESTAURANT**
U.S. 31, Beulah, 882-4431
Hours: Daily, 11a.m. to 9p.m.

Help us celebrate our
# 70th
# Anniversary
*1922 - 1992*

We're using our 1959
menu one day only

**Saturday
June 13, 1992**

*no take-out orders at 1959 prices*

Just imagine: 1959 prices for one day. That's how Cherry Hut celebrated its 70th anniversary!

## The CHERRY HUT
### Beulah *Menu* Michigan

**OUTDOOR DINING SERVING 10 TO 10**

| | |
|---|---|
| Delicious Homemade Soup - Croutons | 35 |
| Turkey Salad Plate - Homemade Rolls | 95 |
| Individual Hot Chicken Pie - Lettuce Salad | 75 |
| Two Homemade Dinner rolls - Butter | 15 |
| Two Homemade Cinnamon Rolls - Butter | 20 |

**SANDWICHES**

| | |
|---|---|
| Sliced Turkey | 70 |
| Turkey Salad | 55 |
| Baked Ham | 55 |
| Baked Ham and Cheese | 65 |
| Egg Salad | 40 |
| Grilled Cheese | 35 |
| Cherry Jelly and Peanut Butter | 25 |
| Peanut Butter | 20 |

**SALADS**

| | |
|---|---|
| Cottage Cheese and Pineapple with Homemade Roll | 35 |
| Heart-o'-Lettuce with Homemade Roll | 25 |

**BEVERAGES**

| | |
|---|---|
| Frosted Cherry Ade | 20 |
| Iced Coffee | 15 |
| Iced Tea | 15 |
| Tea or Milk | 10 |
| Coffee Carafe | 15 |

**DESSERTS**

| | |
|---|---|
| Cherry Hut Cherry Pie | 25 |
| Cherry Pie A La Mode | 35 |
| Cherry Sundae | 30 |
| Vanilla or Cherry Dubonnet Ice Cream | 25 |
| Cherry-Ade Float | 35 |
| Whole Cherry Hut Cherry Pie (to take out) | 75 |

Here's the 1959 souvenir menu with a slice of cherry pie for twenty-five cents!

**From Pie Stand to Icon: The 100 Year History of *The Cherry Hut***

During his time there, Warren says he was most impressed by the incredible consistency and quality of the food and the service, and by the systems, processes, and procedures that Leonard put in place. Leonard and Andy had a favorite saying, "There's only one way to do things, and that's the RIGHT way!" There was a system for everything, from making the pies, setting tables, to mopping the floors, and all the staff members were trained to do their jobs exactly the same way.

This consistency was marked by the records that Leonard kept, stretching back for decades: primarily a sales book, in which for each day the restaurant was open was recorded such details as:

- o How many pies baked and sold that day
- o How many customers for breakfast, lunch, and dinner
- o How many wait staff were needed for each shift
- o How many turkeys were roasted that day
- o What the weather was like
- o What else was happening in Beulah and the surrounding communities

Leonard's logbook doesn't miss a detail.

Warren felt very fortunate in his unique position, as a good friend of Andy's, and entrusted to run a large operation while he was still in high school. His time at The Cherry Hut would serve as a remarkable learning experience for the rest of his life.[144]

Newspaper articles about The Cherry Hut often included recipes, such as in the full-page feature article tying in popular author and illustrator Mary Englebreit.[145] The same article quoted Leonard Case Jr. as saying that Michigan produces 75 percent of the United States cherry crop.

The recipe for cherry muffins found there was created by the article's author. However, here is the real recipe for Cherry Hut cherry muffins, from Christy Case:

• • • • • • • • • • • • • • • • • • • • • • • • • • • • • • • • • • • • • • • • • • • • • • • • • • • • • • •

**Cherry Muffins from The Cherry Hut**

6 Cups Flour
1 ½ Cups Sugar
3 Tablespoons Baking Powder
¾ Cup Oil
¾ Teaspoon Salt
2 Tablespoons Cinnamon
3 Eggs (well-beaten)
3 ½ Cups Milk
6 Cups Chopped Cherries
2 Cups Mayo

Mix dry ingredients together, then add well-beaten eggs. Pour in oil, milk and mayo and mix gently just until blended. Stir in cherries.

Line muffin pans and use black handle scoop to drop in muffin mixture.

**CRUMBLE TOPPING**

1 ½ Cups Margarine (Soft)
1 Tablespoon Cinnamon
2 Cups Brown Sugar
3 Cups Flour

Beat ingredients with hand mixer until blended. Top each muffin with about 1 Tablespoon of crumble.

Bake at 350 degrees for 18 minutes. Makes 48 muffins.

## Magazine and Newspaper Mentions:

The *Detroit Free Press* had a two-page feature article about tourist attractions in the state of Michigan, one per county.[146] Naturally, Cherry Hut was the spot for Benzie County.

In August 1999, The Cherry Hut hit the national news once again when it was number one in a list of top ten places for pie in the United States, in a syndicated article in *USA Today*.[147]

1998: Nancy Sundstrom, "Cherry traditions," *Northern Seasons Summer*, July 16, 1998.

Cherry Hut owner Leonard Case (left) stands with his brother, Bill Case.

**Claudia C. Breland**

Andy Case looks on as his father, Leonard, stirs up some jam.

Andy Case (left) and Warren Call strike a pose, wearing Cherry Hut suspenders.

Education continued being a high priority for The Cherry Hut staff. The Cherry Jerry menu for each season always included a list of the staff members, and what high school or college they were attending.[148] This often became a talking point between the customers and the wait staff. By the 1990s (if not before), both Leonard and Brenda Case were known to encourage staff members to sit at tables and do homework if business was slow.[149]

1990 Menu; Cherry Pie $1.45

1999 Menu; Cherry Pie $1.85

# Celebrating Our Staff: 1990s

Deanna Alsup

Brett Appelton

Tiffany Armstrong

Amy Axline

Jeff Bair

Mike Bair

Pam Bair

Stacy Belisle

Becky Bollenberg

Alice Brozofsky

Chris Burlew

Warren Call

Amanda Case

Andrew Case

Bill Case

Lorayne Case

Morgan Case

Adam Chandler

Charissa Clarke

Lindsay Clarke

Rich Cluff

Renae Conrad

Maggie Cole

Morgan Cole

Andrew Cook

Sandra Cook

Doreen Cooper

Landon Cox

Krista Cozart

Casey Crandon

Nick Danford

Sabra Danford

Jessica Dansby

June Deering

Helena Dell

Jessie DuFrane

Sally Durtche

Rochelle Egan

Perry Ely

Melissa Essex

Rachel Finkel

Paul Flynn

Alex Forest

Crystal Franks

Katie Gibson

Lisa Girven

Melissa Goold

Carrie Gray

Heather Gray

Nicole Gray

Susan Hawkins

Amanda Hefferich

Jamie Henning

Erin Hively

Kay Holt

Hillary Hopkins

Charles Hoppe

Abby Hoyt

Caitlin Hughes

Corey Humes

Harmony Irwin

Holly Jackson

Jenny Johnsen

Lisa Johnson

Rebecca Johnson

Winona Jones

Chris Joy

Minda Kelley

Daniel Kinske

Kathleen Kinske

Angela Knauer

Loraine Laguire

Kallie Lesch

Brenda Lewis

Beulah Loewen

Dawn Lopez

Kelly Lopez

Teresa Loranger

Scott Loree

Lauren Ludwig

Shelly Mahoney

Angie Maidens

Brian Maidens

Mark Makey

Matt Malecki

Pam Marek

Jenny Marshall

Tim Mauntler

Barb McClure

Alison McDonald

Kim Merriman

CONTINUED ON NEXT PAGE

Michelle Merriman

Mark Messina

Robert Mills

Aaron Morden

Bonnie Morten

Shirley Mortenson

Amy Mowrer

Gilbert Murphy

Mariah Myers

Kimberly Needham

Bill Nelson

Melissa Nelson

Nick Nelson

James Norby

Nicole Olney

Michael Olson

Eric Osborn

Ryan Osborn

Mary-Jane Overlease

Christy Putney

Eric Quine

Colleen Rakoczy

Billie Reed

Terri Reed

B.J. Reffit

Julie Reynolds

Sara Rigsbee

Amy Roberts

Phyllis Robinson

Mary Rodriguez

Alison Rosaen

Michelle Royer

Linda Rushing

Christina Ryan

Sandra Saxton

Allison Scarbrough

Nicole Schimke

Renee Schimke

Helen Scott

Erin Showers

Rebecca Spaulding

Nancy Steel

Zachary Taylor

Mark Tolosa

Tami Tolosa

Sara Trowbridge

Ada Truelsson

Kim VanAelst

Wanda Vanderly

Carla VanFarowe

Rick Van Hammen

Matt Wallace

Kary-Ann Waukazoo

Polly Welch

Erin Wells

David Wentzloff

Heather West

Michelle White

Joe Wilson

Tabitha Wilson

Valerie Wingert

Carrie Wynegar

# 2000 to 2009

## Highlights of the New Century:

- **2001:** Andrew Case married Christy Gaylord
- **2002:** Latest edition of *Roadfood* featured Cherry Hut's cherry pie on the cover
- **2003:** Cherry Hut profiled in a feature article in the *New York Times*
- **2004:** Cherry Hut completely remodeled; new dining room, patio, bakery and kitchen added

- **2006:** Cherry Hut voted Business of the Year by Benzie County Chamber of Commerce
- **2008:** Cherry Hut launched its first website
- **2008:** Carson Leonard Case was born

**The first printed recognition of The Cherry Hut** during this decade was reported in the *Benzie County Record-Patriot* of 19 April 2000, which stated that readers of AAA's *Michigan Living* magazine chose The Cherry Hut as one of Michigan's Best Treasures.

For two years in a row, *New York Times* food writer R.W. Apple Jr. wrote about The Cherry Hut in feature articles. In a 2003 feature story, "Up North: Michigan's Flavorful Vacationland," he described how the cherries are harvested by machines, chilled in cold water and then rushed to the local canning and freezing plants. At roadside stands you can buy tart Montmorency cherries (too fragile to ship) and Balaton morellos, recently introduced from Hungary, as well as sweet cherries. At The Cherry Hut, cherry pies were selling for $5.95, but could go up to $6.50 next year.[150]

The following year saw a story called "In the Midwest, a Sweet Tooth is Nonpartisan," in which he describes a memorable visit to The Cherry Hut and a conversation with Brenda Case. She told him the recipe for cherry pie was the original, using lard but no cornstarch, with fresh local cherries in season.[151]

**Other notable newspaper and magazine articles included:**

"Great cherry pie search ends at Beulah 'Hut'" (*Traverse City Record-Eagle*, July 30, 2001)

"12 Hot Spots on the Way Up North," (*Detroit News*, July 13, 2005)

"Cherry Hut's cherry pie receives national acclaim, again," (*Manistee News Advocate*, June 23, 2005)

"Best Reasons to Hit the Road," (*Reader's Digest*, July 2009)

"10 great places to eat regionally, eat well," (*USA Today*, July 24, 2009)

"Cherry Hut rated in upper crust," (*Traverse City Record-Eagle*, June 25, 2005)

In November 2002, the *Lansing State Journal* celebrated the 25th anniversary of the publication of *Roadfood* by Jane and Michael Stern with a feature article and interview with the authors.[152] This particular edition featured a photo of Cherry Hut's famous cherry pie on the front cover. The Cherry Hut made its way to Oprah Winfrey's *O Magazine*, in an article about the best things to eat in every state, and it was a frequent visitor to the pages of *Traverse Magazine*.

This 25th anniversary edition of *Roadfood* features a cover photo of The Cherry Hut's famous cherry pie.

As always, the status of the cherry crop was front-page news in northern Michigan. In June 2002, the *Traverse City Record-Eagle* reported in "Cherry farmers brace for worst," that "the region was expected to produce 3 million pounds this season, compared to 183 million last year."[153]

In July 2003, several articles in Michigan papers highlighted the problems that resulted from a poor crop of cherries. The *Detroit Free Press* had a front-page article titled "State cherry crop at risk," featuring two photographs of The Cherry Hut.[154] It stated that the previous year's crop of only 15 million pounds was "the worst in Michigan history." As a result, prices for cherry products were going up by as much as 10 percent. The Cherry Hut was always able to obtain their cherries locally due to their long-standing relationships with local farmers and cherry producers.

In the *Port Huron Times Herald* of July 7, 2003, the article "For Grand Traverse farmers, life is just a crop of cherries," reported that Michigan's cherry crop would be smaller this year, driving prices up. Damaged by a February thaw and a wet, cold spring, the cherries suffered. Each week The Cherry Hut goes through about 3000 pounds of cherries to make 500 pies.

In 2004, The Cherry Hut was completely remodeled, adding a new dining room, patio, bakery and kitchen.[155] Bringing the restaurant into the future, it also included a nod to its past, in the murals painted in the dining room (the hard work of Casey Crandon) and the old photos on the walls.[156] A bulletin board outside Andy's office held the current Benzie Central High School's Honor Roll, with names of staff members highlighted in red.[157] At this point, during the summer season Cherry Hut could see up to 500 guests in a day.

Former staffer Kayla (Kermode) Six remembers:

*Working at The Cherry Hut was one of my first official jobs. I started as a "Salad Maker," then donned the signature red and white striped dress and became a Cherry Hut waitress. Looking back, I am impressed with the professional manner with which the Case family managed The Cherry Hut. From Day One, I was trained not only to complete the job of making salads or waiting tables, but to do so while adhering to high standards and impeccable etiquette. When making salads, I learned to make salads with the correct ingredients and in a consistent, aesthetically pleasing way (there was a specific style, order and placement to every ingredient!). I remember Andy Case emphasizing that a customer should be able to expect the same dish in both presentation and quality every time they visited The Cherry Hut. The same rigor and expectation applied to waiting tables. I went through a three-day training session with Brenda Case that would make Emily Post proud. The training covered everything from basic serving skills, common courtesy and professional diction when conversing with customers, specific ways to serve each dish or drink, the timing with which to serve a dish or check on a table, and an overall standard of execution and excellence. I carry many of these skills and practices into my professional and personal life today. I can still make a gorgeous salad when friends come for dinner and the habit of adhering to a high standard in every aspect of work has served me well in my post-collegiate career.*

*During my years at The Cherry Hut, the Case family exemplified true leadership. I remember several instances where The Cherry Hut was extremely busy during the peak months of July or August and the kitchen, serving and bussing staff were all overwhelmed by the demand. The Case family, without missing a beat, would jump in to support the staff. Brenda would grab a notepad and serve the newly seated table, Christy and Leonard donned aprons and began bussing tables, and Andy, dressed in a white button-down shirt and tie, would throw his tie over his shoulder and begin building sandwiches, making salads or starting the next batch of french fries. The "bosses" were not there to boss the employees around. Rather, the Cases were true leaders who knew The Cherry Hut business down to the way to serve the obscure menu item or the exact ingredients for the club sandwich. Not only that, but they were willing to step in to support their staff, even if that meant clearing dirty dishes and ending the day with gravy on their clothes.*

Leonard Case—the parade's Grand Marshal in 2003—waves to the crowd.

Cherry Hut staffers are ready for the parade.

## Celebrating Our Staff: 2000 to 2009

| | | | |
|---|---|---|---|
| Cassandra Acton | Dana Baun | Elizabeth Bonhorst | Adrienne Call |
| Cheryl Andrews | Cindy Beckowitz | | Mariah Call |
| Donita Andrews | Stephen Beckowitz | Kelly Boyce | Warren Call |
| Lexi Andrews | | Miranda Brandon | Jamie Carnes |
| Karen Atkinson | Lowell Berryhill | | Justin Carter |
| Lee Atkinson | Paul Blough | Johnna Braun | |
| Maggie Atkinson | Ryan Blough | Melissa Burch | CONTINUED ON NEXT PAGE |
| Whitney Ayers | Hadley Boehm | Carmen Burzynski | |

CONTINUED ON NEXT PAGE

Amanda Case

Andrew Case

Christy Case

Lorayne Case

Robert Centlivre

Britta Cicansky

Charissa Clarke

Jessica Compton

Doreen Cooper

Phyllis Crowell-VanHammen

Joan Culbertson

Katie Curtis

Lynn Czarnecki

Courtney Czehawksi

Ashley Conger

Andrew Cook

Sabra Danford

Jeanette Dennis

Kara Derry

Lindsey Dobbins

D.J. DuFrane

Jessie DuFrane

Milana Duggan

Marcy Dunlap

Carol Dye

Katie Edinger

Jonathan Ehman

Kelsey Elliot

Perry Ely

Kyle Esch

Nathan Esch

Jake Fekete

Albert Fella

Darwyn Fishinghawk

Sabra Fitzgerald

Nancy Fleetwood

Paul Flynn

Jamie Fortin

Olivia Fought

Nick Fowler

Chris Frostic

Katie Gibson

Megan Goodchild

Missy Goold

Brooke Gray

Carrie Gray

Mikaela Gray

Shana Gunther

Donovan Haase

Noah Hahn

Carol Hammond

Wanda Hancock

Christina Harig

Melanie Harig

Corey Harrison

Mitchell Harrison

Julie Heacock

Kim Heacock

Alec Heinrich

Michael Heltzel

Scott Hendrix

Stephanie Hendrix

Cassie Henry

Noreen Henry

Kay Holt

Philip Holt

Garry Honeycutt

Hillary Hopkins

Abby Hoyt

Caitlin Hughes

Rebecca Hughes

Jannine James

Kristen Jansens

Justin Jewell

Aaron Johnson

Leah Johnson

Michael Johnson

Rory Johnson

Cortney Jones

Winona Jones

Doug Joy Jr.

Victoria Joy

Daniel Karner

Adam Kaskinen

**CONTINUED ON NEXT PAGE**

Joel Kaskinen

Robert Kerby

Kayla Kermode

Luke Kermode

Patricia Kinske

Hanna Knudson

Eric Koch

Samantha Kosiboski

Shayla Kulwaiak

Deborah LaGuire

Jeannie LaDuke

Beau Lamont

Nadine Lamont

Cassidy Larimer

Hannah Leonhardt

Elizabeth Liakopoulos

Matthew Lloyd

John Lowe

Lauren Ludwig

Brian Maidens

Courtney Marshall

Neil Marshall

Melissa Martin

Barb McClure

Nicole McDonald

Katie McKeever

Cheyenne McMillion

Isabella Merrill

Krystyna Messersmith

Brandon Mikowski

Meredith Milarch

Mason Moody

Aaron Morden

Abbey Moreno-Gaft

Zachary Motzler

Amy Mowrer

Moriah Myers

Ravenna Myers

Bill Nelson

Nick Nelson

Cameron Neveu

Kelsey Neveu

Kim Nolf

James Norby

Whitney Nowak

Donald Omar

Eric Osborn

Ryan Osborn

A.J. Patterson

Lynn Patterson

Sharlene Patterson

Matt Potter

Ashley Puccio

Lauren Putney

Ingrid Radionoff

R.J. Rafferty

Diana Reed

Terri Reed

Jessica Rhodes

Hannah Rodriguez

Ashley Rosaen

Chris Rothhaar

Brian Samonie

Amanda Sanchez

Cindy Sauer

Lauren Saffron

Sandra Saxton

Heidi Schaub

Amanda Scheele

Megan Schoen

Helen Scott

Kristen Spalding

David Sparks

Judy Stafford

Roxann Stevens

Paula Stolz

Jamie Swarthwood

Sarah Tarsney

**CONTINUED ON NEXT PAGE**

## Celebrating Our Staff: **2000 to 2009 (continued)**

Jay Teegardin

Erin Thompson

Hannah Thompson

Mary Thompson

Ryan Thompson

Thomas Thompson

Alex Turland

Kassie Turner

Mike VanAntwerp

Ian VanDeperre

Dave Van Hammen

Katie Van Hammen

Rick Van Hammen

David VanHorn

Matt Verstrat

Linda Vincent

Matt Wallace

Christy Warfield

Tracy Warfield

Samantha Weaver

Gregory Weisbrodt

Tim Wentzloff

Kaitlin Winder

Judy Wisser

Theresa Wojtoaricz

Monique Wylie

# 2010 to Present

**Highlights of the New Decade:**

- **2012:** Caleb James Case was born
- **2013:** Cherry Hut featured in a PBS documentary about the Leelanau Peninsula entitled "Fork in the Road"
- **2013:** James Kraker Jr. dies
- **2014:** Cherry Hut starts shipping fresh baked pies
- **2015:** Cherry Hut in Benzonia is remodeled
- **2016:** Leonard Leach Case Jr. dies
- **2017:** Brenda Joy Case dies

**Leonard Leach Case Jr. died in Beulah on April 16, 2016,** after a lifetime of creating jams and jellies for The Cherry Hut, and having been the owner since 1960. "During his time as owner, Leonard transformed The Cherry Hut from an outdoor food stop with a limited menu only open for 12 weeks in the summer months, to a modern three dining room restaurant with a full menu of entrees, sandwiches and salads, which is open Mother's Day until the end of October."[158]

Fortunately, both Leonard and Brenda lived long enough to enjoy the newest generation of Cherry Hutters in their grandsons Carson Leonard Case and Caleb James Case. True to tradition, as soon as the boys were old enough, they began helping out in the Hut. It was also very important to Leonard that he travel to meet his third grandson, Zach Williford, born in North Carolina May 2015 to Amanda Williford Case and her husband Ashley Williford. A fourth grandson, Gabe Williford, was born in April 2019. They are frequent visitors of The Cherry Hut and even though they don't reside in northern Michigan, they will always be a part of The Cherry Hut family.

Andy remembers how fanatical his father was about the ice cream. He would really get after the waitresses if he felt they were putting too much ice cream on the pie or for sundaes. He would look at the finished product (i.e., pie à la mode and sundaes before they went out into the dining room) and comment "there go all the profits." He also did not like having the window blinds down. He called them the "closed signs" and would prefer they were open even if the sun was glaring right into someone's eyes. When he would see some staff members standing around in a group not getting a lot done, he would quip "1 person gets all the work done, 2 people each get half of the work done, and 3 people get none of the work done."

Ned Edwards recalls:

> The Benzonia Congregational Church was packed and overflowing with relatives, friends, admirers and Cherry Hutters when Leonard was memorialized there. Everyone knew him in Benzie County, not only as the owner of The Cherry Hut, but also as the boy who grew up in Benzonia; son of the Justice of the Peace; named "Business Man of the Year" by the Chamber of Commerce; and perhaps the only person in Michigan to grow and operate a restaurant successfully without a liquor license. Andy spoke eloquently-but-humorously about his father at the service, telling of Leonard's refusal to put more than one scoop of ice cream on a piece of cherry pie à la mode. At the end of the service, Andy invited everyone in the church to come down to The Cherry Hut for a piece of pie with two scoops of ice cream on it! They did, and it was a wonderful celebration of Leonard's life, for he had been proprietor of the Hut for 56 years! People will not forget his personal style of stopping by their table at The Cherry Hut to chat and find out "how you doin'."[159]

Thus, Andy took over the ownership and proprietorship of The Cherry Hut, beginning a new era of innovation and leadership. He brought with him a transformed logo: Cherry Jerry with arms and legs, new gifts at the counter and new treats on the menu. But the wonderful pies, turkey sandwiches and dinner continue, along with the decades of Cherry Hut tradition.

Three generations of the Case family.

Leonard Case at
The Cherry Hut.

**Claudia C. Breland**

Brenda Case

Caleb Case
assembling pies.

**From Pie Stand to Icon: The 100 Year History of** *The Cherry Hut*

## Magazine Mentions

Jane and Michael Stern, "Life in the Slow Lane," *Gourmet*, February 2000, p.53.

"The Cherry Hut of Beulah, Michigan, hasn't changed in decades. We ate this particular piece of pie during a late-summer visit in 1978."

Jenny Gavacs, "Gee Whiz, Cherries!" *Traverse*, June 2000, (insert) BM 15.

"The Cherry Hut serves the same purpose as '50s soda shops — food, friends and seasonal jobs."

Jane and Michael Stern, "In the Pie of the Beholder," *Gourmet*, September 2002, 71.

"To those who have spent any time traveling Route 31 along Lake Michigan's eastern shore, The Cherry Hut has become as familiar a feature of the landscape as the orchards themselves."

Paul Lukas, "The Ultimate Pie-Tinerary," *Money*, September 2003, p.132.

"...where the excellent pie comes topped with a generous dollop of Americana."

Jane and Michael Stern, "A Guide to America's Best Roadfood," *Gourmet*, November 2003, supplement, p.11

"Comfort food lunch is grand at this 1920s vintage roadside eatery, but pie baked with locally grown cherries is the destination dish."

Patty LaNoue Stearns, "Dining," *Traverse*, May 2004, p.63.

"Jerry the pie-faced boy has presided over this kitschy former fruit stand since 1922."

Meeta Agrawal, "Pie Chart: In Search of America's Best," *Life*, 1 July 2005, p.10.

"Cherries are one of the season's greatest treats..."

Patty LaNoue Stearns, "Up North Classics," *Traverse*, July 2005, p.77.

> "The 50's look, the all-American fare and Jerry the pie-faced mascot — that's why tourists flock here May through October for a taste of kitsch with their sweet cherry pie."

Sarah McColl with Andrew Knowlton, "Destination USA: The United Plates of America," *Bon Appetit*, May 2009, p.82.

> "What to Eat: A slice of cherry pie at The Cherry Hut Restaurant."

Jane and Michael Stern, "Best Reasons to Hit the Road," *Reader's Digest*, July 2009, p.74. "... five all-time favorites, from *500 Things to Eat Before It's Too Late...*"

> "At America's fruit pie mecca, each unwieldy serving is one quarter of a whole pie..."

Christy Case, "Cherry Hut Veggie Quiche," *Traverse*, September 2017, p.81.

> "Leave it to the family behind Benzie County's iconic Cherry Hut restaurant to excel at anything baked in a crust."

2012: Robert Fitzke, "Cherry Hut marks its 60th," *Traverse City (Mich.) Record-Eagle*, 29 August 2012. (note: it's actually 90th anniversary) History of cherries in Michigan. French colonists brought cherries and planted them in Canada & along St. Lawrence River & into Great Lakes. In 1852 Pete Dougherty planted a small orchard of cherry trees on the Old Mission Peninsula, which thrived.

2019: Ross Boissoneau, "Beulah's Cherry Hut," *Northern Express*, 1 July 2019, p.16.

> "Staff members include Chris Petritz, Mimi Appel, their sister Dosie Kermode's daughter Kayla Six, and "one mom, her two daughters and four cousins."

# Celebrating Our Staff: 2010 to Present

Cheryl Andrews

Donita Andrews

Lexi Andrews

Whitney Ayers

Allison Baker

Kayla Bates

Cathy Beltz

Rachelle Bishop

Ramsey Blough

Zachariah Blough

Melissa Burch

Morgan Burch

Peyton Burch

Riley Burch

Caleb Case

Carson Case

Britta Cicansky

Shelby Clark

Alisha Clous

Victoria Cobb

Andrew Cook

Donald Crossman Jr.

Sabra Danford

Cynthia Dansby

RandiJo Dault-Johnson

Mercedes Deeren

Ferdinand deGuia

Dayanara Dennis

Autumn DeRidder

Christian Dilas

Morgan Donally

Colton Downs

Brianna DuFrane

Brendan Duggan

Danielle Duggan

Milana Duggan

Ryan Duggan

Bethany Dunlap

Hayley Dunlop

Beck Edwards

Jessie Einhorn-Johnson

Cassandra Ely

Perry Ely

Kyle Esch

Hailey Fiel

Alyson Fink

Breanna Fink

Kyle Fink

McKenna Fink

Nancy Fleetwood

Mikenna Flohe

Nicholas Fowler

James Fritz

Jeff Gaft

Anya Gau

Ella Gaylord

Whitney Gibbs

Megan Goodchild

Sara Goodchild

Jason Goold

Melissa Goold

David Gosma

Katherine Gossens

Katie Gottardo

Tianna Gould

Joshua Gray

Hailey Guinan

Ismael Halaweh

Dale Hansen

Matthew Harrington

Savannah Hayden

Chad Hedrick

Elizabeth Heinz

Stephanie Hendrix

Emmy Hill

Chandler Holley

Kay Holt

Isabella Huddleston

Jordan Hunt

CONTINUED ON NEXT PAGE

Malia Jackson

Kristen Jansens

Alexis Johnson

Doug Joy Jr.

Victoria Joy

Cora Kangas

Emma Kangas

Adam Kaskinen

Joel Kaskinen

Kevin Keipert

Kayla Kermode

Christopher Knapp

Eric Koch

AuSable Kreiner

Canaan Kreiner

Jacob Kruty

Abby Lafferty

Ann Latrell

Hannah Leonhardt

Danielle Lepor

Daisy Leuenberger

Karen MacGirr

Brian Maidens

Cecile Mallon

Frances Mapes-Pearson

Andrew Marshall

Claire Marshall

Courtney Marshall

Molly Marshall

Neil Marshall

Lyle Martell

Jacob Maue

Hayley May

Elsa Merrill

Hannah Messersmith

James Messersmith

Sarah Middleton

Meredith Milarch

Katelynn Millard

Alison Moore

Kaitlyn Moore

Kayley Moore

Megan Moore

Abby Moreno-Gaft

Max Moreno-Gaft

Allison Moyer

Natalie Moyer

Michael Musgrave

Josiah Myers

Ravenna Myers

Cameron Neveu

Kelsey Neveu

Jacob Niesen

Jennifer Niesen

Rachel Niesen

Hadley O'Connor

Madison O'Connor

Maren O'Connor

Eric Osborn

Katie Osborn

Leslie Osborn

Ryan Osborn

Emma Page

Libby Page

Sierra Pallin

Matthew Parlette

Noelle Parlette

A.J. Patterson

Lynn Patterson

Sharlene Patterson

Alexis Perry

Zachery Perry

Austin Potts

Katelyn Pruyne

Jordin Purchase

Debra Reed

**CONTINUED ON NEXT PAGE**

Jacob Reed

Luke Reed

Alex Reitzel

Lucas Richards

Troy Richley

Hannah Rodriguez

Christopher Rothhaar

David Sale

Cynthia Sauer

Dylan Sauer

Monika Schafer

Heidi Schaub

Jessica Schaub

Earl Schopp

Tammy Sedlar-Wing

Kendahl Serrano

Lauren Serrano

Lynette Skimin

Timothy Skimin

Brianna Smith

Kyle Smith

Nevaeh Smith

Corinna Snow

Jasper Snow

Judith Stafford

Joseph Stain

John Stepanovich

Haley Stephan

Roxann Stevens

Paula Stolz

Sarah Stolz

Larisa Stone

Sandra Straubel

Kendra Stuck

Liam Tabora-Jones

Allison Tayer

Regan Terry

Erin Thompson

LeeAnn Tincher

Rebecca Towersey

Rhonda Trombly

Jordan Turner

Katie Van Hammen

Rick Van Hammen

Carla VanFarowe

Marya VanFarowe

Wesley VanPoortfliet

Arielle Wade

Taylor Weatherholt

Samantha Weaver

Timothy Wing

Laurel Wolfe-Waurzynek

Andrew Wolowiec

Jamie Yeager

Taylor Zolman

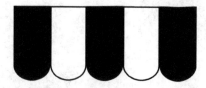

# Unprecedented Times: 2020-2022

**From Cherry Jerry's newsletter, Spring 2020:**

Greetings from northern Michigan

Well folks, it's been quite a spring up here. If we could sum this up, we would, but like many of you across the country it's hard to make sense of everything that is occurring. We thought we would break it down into two categories for you. We'll call it, what we don't know and what we do know.

**What we don't know:**
- When we'll be opening for the year. Our original opening date was set for Saturday, May 9th. We want to be optimistic, but don't foresee that happening at this time.
- What our dining experience will look like. We would like nothing more than to see as many smiling faces as possible, but we don't know what that looks like in the context of the current environment.

**What we do know:**
- We are so thankful for our healthcare workers and essential workers. They are doing a fantastic job!
- The Cherry Hut will be open at some point for our 98th season.
- Restaurants are closed until April 30th in Michigan.
- We are still shipping our packaged and jarred goods via cherryhut.com
- When we do open, it will be after we get guidance of relevant regulations from government authorities.

- We have and will continue to abide by health department regulations to ensure you and yours a meaningful and safe Cherry Hut experience.
- We started as a stand on the shore of Crystal Lake selling pies and have now grown into a full-service restaurant and gift shop that delivers smiles all over America. The virus won't ever change that. Please know that our intent is to provide you as much as we can in our upcoming season! The Cherry Hut has survived the Great Depression, the second World War and numerous other recessions and disasters. We've made it this long, not because of us, but because you've supported us over the years. Our collective resolve will get us through this. Thanks for your continued support and patronage!

We'll write more when we know more! Stay safe and stay healthy!

**Cherry On,**
**Cherry Jerry**
**& The Case Family**

Cherry Jerry masks up during the 2020 pandemic.

**Claudia C. Breland**

The first hint of things to come was in a small two-sentence item in the January 4, 2020 *Seattle Times* leading with "Mystery disease."[160] The outbreak of coronavirus in the United States began in several nursing homes in Western Washington, brought by international travelers from China; at the end of February 2020 there were 60 reported cases in the United States.[161]

The first outbreak in Michigan was reported in March 2020, and on March 16, Governor Gretchen Whitmer ordered all bars and restaurants to close to sit-down dining.[162] Because The Cherry Hut was a seasonal restaurant, open only during the summer, it escaped being closed.

Andy explained that:

> At the onset of the pandemic the state of Michigan closed all indoor dining until Memorial Day Weekend of 2020. That year we did not open until Father's Day weekend. Then The Cherry Hut was open every day after until our normal close date of the third Sunday in October.
>
> Thankfully, when the state of Michigan closed restaurants again for indoor dining late in 2020, we had already closed for the season. We were fortunate in that regard. During the pandemic years of 2020 and 2021 we were still extremely busy. We field an extreme number of take-out orders, which has been challenging since that was really not a big part of our business in the past. Hopefully, take out winds down somewhat, since I don't believe the "Cherry Hut Experience" is a turkey plate in a plastic container. It is the sit-down experience and ambiance and history of a meal in the dining room.

However, in 2021 due to a record amount of people coming to northern Michigan, and suffering from the same labor shortages as others in the hospitality business we had to shorten some hours. Especially, last fall (2021) when we only served lunch daily 11 a.m.–4 p.m. and did not open for any dinner service. That's never happened in the past. Also, part of the challenge is we have never been so busy in the fall either. Usually, in the fall season we could get by with a smaller staff, but no longer. So, we had to circle the wagons and put everyone on to take care of just the 11–4 period.

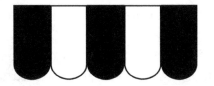

# The Cherry Hut
## Today

How The
Cherry Hut
looks today!

Andy and Christy Case, Proprietors

Ryan Osborn, Manager, Oversees both the Restaurant and Benzonia Store
Neil Marshall, Assistant Manager
Kay Holt, Assistant Manager
Rick Van Hammen, Kitchen Manager

**The Cherry Hut has always been an important part** of the community in Beulah and the surrounding area. For years, the managers have hosted Chamber of Commerce meetings, hosted visits from elementary school students, and donated jams and jellies for good causes.

"Thankfully, The Cherry Hut has been consistently busy every year that my memory goes back," said owner Andy Case. "We have been so fortunate in that regard. I would like to think it is due to a consistently good product, with friendly and professional service, in a clean and welcoming environment. I think now that we have so many years under our belt that the long history of The Cherry Hut plays a large part (i.e., our grandparents came here, as did my parents, and now so do I...). I believe almost more than the food, The Cherry Hut is selling a "memory of northern Michigan." It's quite a unique place.

"We have never had to lay off any employees. Pretty much the opposite, we are always looking for more 'Cherry Jerry's Helpers' to help serve the many Cherry Hutters looking for a meal!"[163]

Much of Cherry Hut's fresh produce, meat and dairy are locally sourced; the thirty-pound lugs of five to one cherries come from Smeltzer Orchards in Frankfort.[164] The tradition of serving roast turkey, which began in 1936, goes back to the days when the Marshall family had a turkey farm in Benzie County.[165] The menu features homemade soups daily with a soup and sandwich special named after Andy and Christy's oldest son, Carson, in addition to Caleb's homemade quiche named after Andy and Christy's youngest son, Caleb, and made with the famous Cherry Hut pie crust. Fresh roast turkey is part of many items on the menu including "The Original Turkey Sandwich," a turkey cranberry Havarti sandwich, a hot turkey sandwich with homemade mashed potatoes, the turkey pot pie, or you can have it as an addition to a variety of fresh salads. The turkey has almost become just as popular as the cherry at The Cherry Hut!

During the height of the summer season (generally July and August), The Cherry Hut kitchen goes through at least 500 pounds of flour per week—and that's just for the pies. This does not count flour used for other baked goods such as cinnamon rolls or muffins. They roast as many as eight turkeys a day to keep up with the demand for the roast turkey dinners offered on the menu during the whole season. The record for the number of pies baked in one day is a whopping 640; former staffer Warren Call remembers getting 300 pies baked before the restaurant opened every morning.[166]

It should be obvious by now that, more than anything else, The Cherry Hut revolves around families. From the earliest days of the Kraker and Rogers families and their deep involvement in the cherry orchards of Benzie County, to the present-day owners Andy and Christy Case and their sons, it's been about family all this time. Many families in the Grand Traverse area have contributed multiple generations of staffers: the Cases, the Marshalls, the Wolfes (at this time, nineteen Wolfe descendants have been staffers), the Van Hammens, the Calls, the Bairs, the Trapps, and the list goes on. This speaks to the intergenerational loyalty and affection some families have toward The Cherry Hut. We have heard from many customers who are now taking fourth- and fifth-generation family members to enjoy the quality atmosphere and delicious food at The Cherry Hut. As former staffer Angela explained:

*They've kept busy baking and serving 300–400 pies each day, topping 500 in the peak weeks of summer. The recipe is consistent with their history; it hasn't changed since 1922, even with remodeling jobs and updates. They've maintained their identity, their homey All-American menu and quality of service, and the feeling that everything's right with the world when you lay down your fork.*[167]

Jenny Marshall noted that the Donald Marshall family has a rich history with The Cherry Hut.

*The current "Hutters" are the fourth generation working to contribute to The Cherry Hut experience. There have been 14 of us on The Cherry Hut team at some point in our lives, with a combined 67 years of service. Needless to say, the Marshall family has been significant to The Cherry Hut. But The Cherry Hut has been equally important to the Marshall family. What does The Cherry Hut mean to the Marshalls?*

*That is answered with just one word—family.*

Four generations of the Donald Marshall family have worked at The Cherry Hut.

**Claudia C. Breland**

For each Marshall, working at The Cherry Hut means spending time with family. When you are working alongside sisters, brothers, cousins, your mom, or aunt, it is family time. Our summer evenings end with a sharing of the day's events at The Cherry Hut. Believe me when I say that we are never without a story! For example, who in the world tries to eat a hot turkey sandwich by picking it up instead of using a knife and fork? Each night, laughter fills the Marshall "compound" as a Cherry Hut story like this is shared with siblings, cousins, parents and grandparents.

And the idea of family goes beyond bloodlines for employees at The Cherry Hut. As summers pass at The Cherry Hut, you develop familial relationships with co-workers and the guests in the restaurant. You know when graduations and engagements happen, changing the makeup of the Hut family. You feel the heartbreak of a spouse, who finds themselves now dining alone. You witness new babies joining families, anxious for them to have that first taste of our famous pie.

Each summer builds on the last and you become a part of each other's lives in an intimate way. Family is a word that defines the spirit of being part of The Cherry Hut. For the Marshalls, we have been blessed to enjoy time with family both physically and in spirit because of summers working at The Cherry Hut.

Assistant manager Neil Marshall said that although grounded in some very firm traditions, "The Cherry Hut has certainly evolved over the years, and Andy and Christy have done a masterful job of managing this evolution."

New menu items pop up every season, while the famous cherry pie remains unchanged. The indoor dining area has expanded significantly, but it is still possible to enjoy your Cherry Hut favorites under a classic red-and-white umbrella while seated at a patio table. The bakery and kitchen areas have been enlarged and modernized, but the same pie ovens visible in the background of all those "historic" photos of The Cherry Hut from the Forties and Fifties are still being fired up every morning. Each day when I come to work, I open the door to the heavenly aroma of turkeys roasting and pies and cinnamon rolls baking. There isn't a much better way to begin a day—unless, of course, you are walking in the front door of The Cherry Hut and being seated at a table ready to order some of that roast turkey and pie and cinnamon rolls! Hope to see all of you doing just that again very soon.

Cherry Hut Products in Benzonia, Michigan, has a long-standing tradition of shipping homemade jams and jellies throughout the country, said Andy Case. He continued:

*Leonard Case Jr. learned many recipes from James Kraker in the 1950s and personally made many of the products until Leonard's son Andy took over jam making duties from him in 2004. Leonard still helped make jam up until his passing in 2016. All jars have always been hand poured and capped with no added artificial flavoring or preservatives. Leonard himself poured over 1,000,000 jars in his lifetime. Most of the many different flavors are sold out of the restaurant in Beulah, but many more are shipped out in gift boxes for enjoyment across the USA. Also, The Cherry Hut wholesales their jams to stores in Michigan and other states.*

The Cherry Hut in Benzonia warms up a cold winter day.

**Claudia C. Breland**

Some of the original flavors such as Sweet Cherry Conserve and Pure Cherry Preserves still carry over to today. Others such as Crabapple Jelly, Plum Jelly, Red Currant Jelly, and Quince Jelly among others have ceased to be produced as demand waned and appetites increased for more cherry products. New flavors such as Cherry Berry, Reduced Sugar Cherry Jam, and Cherry Pepper Jelly have taken their place. The Cherry Hut ships out large quantities of jams throughout the year, but most are shipped during the busy Christmas season. Everyone, especially all The Cherry Hutters out there, like to ship a little reminder of their memory and trip to northern Michigan. And that reminder is in the form of a Cherry Hut Cherry Jam!

The Cherry Hut storeroom—a far cry from the early days
of the roadside stand.

**From Pie Stand to Icon: The 100 Year History of** *The Cherry Hut*

The Cherry Hut...making Christmas shopping easy.

Here are some memories from long-time staffer Ryan Osborn:

*Mystery*

*Earlier in my years at The Cherry Hut I was responsible for vacuuming the floors of the dining room. This would take place in the morning before the restaurant opened for food service. Day after day I was able to perform this task without bother or interruption as I was, for the most part, alone. The dining area had been empty since the night before. The tables and chairs had been cleaned and set aside to make the room ready for vacuuming, nothing but the occasional half-eaten dinner roll or abandoned crayon had been left behind. I always considered the ritual to be exercise and meditation to start the day.*

*One morning, as I began sweeping the dining room, I noticed a large shiny object under one of the booths. When I picked up the coin, I was surprised by the weight of it and quickly inspected it to find that it was a silver dollar! Not only did I find a nearly mint silver dollar, but it was also a 1922 silver dollar! Immediately, I had the feeling that this coin was a little extra special and anyone that had misplaced it would be sure glad to have it back. I took the coin first to the owner of The Cherry*

Hut, but Leonard assured me that the coin was not his and told me that "some folks carry those around for good luck, maybe it fell out of a pocket." Over the next couple of days, I was able to ask each of my coworkers if they had lost the coin—all denied ownership. It was October so the end of the season was near for The Cherry Hut, but I kept the coin at the restaurant in case the owner came to claim it. No one ever did come to ask if we had found their lucky silver coin. So, it is kind of a mystery as to how this coin ended up on the floor of The Cherry Hut dining room. Maybe a guest lost it and then wrote it off as "lost." Maybe the building had been holding it for years until it rolled from the rafters. Maybe "Cherry Jerry" placed it there for some fortunate person to find it.

*Relationship Secret*

One of my favorite truths about The Cherry Hut is its ability to form and keep relationships. Relationships between coworkers are easily formed due to the positive and pleasant environment that exists throughout the entire building, from the beginning of each day to the very end. Really, who could drive right pass the giant smiling Cherry Jerry, on their way into work, and then walk into the back door an unlikable grouch?!? Relations between employer and employee are created and kept starting with a clear and available line of communication. The schedule is simple and flexible which is perfect for busy high school and college students earning money for the school year.

All the favorable features of The Cherry Hut atmosphere led to a terrific relationship between the Hut staff and our guests. The guests are greeted with a smile and are treated like Cherry Hut family whether they are stopping in quick for pie or if they are staying for a complete dinner with friends. Something I have noticed during my years at the Hut, is that the owners like to greet long-time returning guests by their names. With so many guests during our busy summer season, it would be nearly impossible to remember all those names! Unknown to most, there exists a small notebook full of names and descriptions of steadfast visitors. I think this obscure fact is remarkable in an era where if your name ends up on an establishment's list, you're likely going to be shown the door as soon as you've been recognized inside. So, if it is you that happens to be greeted, by name, with a handshake at the door, you very well may be on this list!

Andy Case has been operating The Cherry Hut Restaurant since 1999. However, it has been a part of his life since birth, and he officially started helping out at age 10. He began by putting away dishes on busy days. As he got into high school, his role changed to more of a front-of-the-house role. You would often see him running the cash register and seating customers. Now, as owner of the restaurant, you can still find him out front with customers throughout the day. Even though there are numerous tasks that go into running a full-service restaurant and shipping business, Andy feels that it is very important for the customers to see him working and interacting with the guests whenever possible. In 1995 Andy graduated from high school Magna Cum Laude and carried on his father's tradition of attending Michigan State University where he majored in Hospitality Business Management. Before he graduated from college he was hired as a paid intern to manage two restaurants with the Walt Disney Corporation in Orlando, Florida. After graduation from college, he returned to his hometown to begin managing and operating The Cherry Hut.

Leonard and his son Andy Case at The Cherry Hut.

During his time as manager and eventually owner, the restaurant has been featured in newspapers, magazines, and books, the Food Network and several local news stations. The restaurant has undergone almost a complete remodel along with the products building located in Benzonia, and Andy is continuously looking for ways to modernize while keeping the original All-American feel.

Andy's wife Christy has her own Cherry Hut Story:

*I began taking piano lessons at the age of 7 from Dorothy Rice, whose family was also a known business owner in Benzie County. Dorothy lived just around the lake on Crystal Drive and only just a few miles or so from The Cherry Hut. It was always*

**Claudia C. Breland**

*a highlight for my mother Carolyn and I to stop at The Cherry Hut after piano lessons for a large cinnamon roll and a bowl of cheese soup. We did this frequently until I graduated from high school in 1995. Andy would typically be there running the cash register and seating guests. My mother would always ask me if I wanted to pay, secretly trying to pique my interest in the young man at the cash register. Who would have thought that just years later that cashier would become my husband and that The Cherry Hut would be such an integral part of my life along with our two sons, Carson and Caleb?*

Christy has since taken on a full-time role at The Cherry Hut after teaching music in the public school system for seventeen years. She runs the back of the house and spends much of her time cooking and creating new recipes each year. Sons Carson and Caleb both take part in a generations-long tradition by playing an active role as well: Carson as a dishwasher, host, and third-generation jam maker; and Caleb as a host and master of putting the Cherry Jerry stickers on the pie lids. On many occasions, you will see the entire family working together, interacting with guests and handling the day-to-day operations that help keep The Cherry Hut running smoothly.

The Case family, three generations

# A Century
# of Leadership

Original owners, J.L. and
Dorothy Kraker

Jimmy and Dottie Kraker

George and Althea Kraker Petritz

George and
Althea Petritz
in 1971

George and
Althea Petritz
in the 1980s

Leonard and
Brenda Case

The Andy
Case family

**Claudia C. Breland**

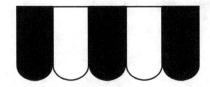

# *Through the Years: Customer Memories*

·····················································································

**From Scott Wagner, Columbus, Ohio:**

We first visited the Crystal Lake region in 1966. My mom, who had spent her summers at Muskegon on her aunt's farm during the Great Depression, loved the northwest region of Michigan and wanted to pass that experience on to my younger brother Bret and I. We stayed at Chimney Corners that first week-long vacation trip, and subsequent years with my parents rented cottages from the wonderful Rev. Gilbert Applehof. The cottages are still on the lake to this day!

As I recall, The Cherry Hut was probably the first restaurant we visited in Beulah. Beulah was a much different place then, a typical small town of the 1960s, with a movie theater, car dealership, drug store and grocery store. The Cherry Hut was distinctly different, and it became a regular stop for us. The additional dining area had not yet been added to The Cherry Hut, so the interior dining area consisted of the section with the A-frame type roof—which is my favorite area to dine in.

While I remember the cherry pie as a youngster, my best memory of The Cherry Hut was the genuine Cherry Hut T-shirts, which remain unchanged to this day. My brother and I got a new one each year as we returned. It was always one of my favorite shirts.

As I grew into a teenager, my interests in life changed. There were many diversions in those days, especially when I got my driver's license and my own car. A lot of years passed without a visit to the lake, which as an adult I regret—what was I thinking?

That all changed when I started bringing my wife up to the lake some 12 years ago. She is totally blind, and because of that, the soothing waves of Crystal Lake and Lake Michigan mean a lot to her, and so do special smells like one finds upon entering The Cherry Hut. I was delighted to find that Cherry Hut (and really most of the region) hadn't changed in all that time.

My wife is much younger than I. Seven years ago she gave me my one and only child, Owen. One of the most important things to me was to introduce him to life at Crystal Lake. Both my wife and son have (in her case surprisingly) adapted to the cool crystal-clear lake water and enjoy swimming in it every year. When Owen turned three, we started spending a full two weeks at the lake. It is our most treasured time of the year. Our very first stop at the lake after our 7-hour drive from Ohio, is for late lunch or early dinner, at The Cherry Hut—and one of eventually several pies leaves with us—along with Owen's newest Cherry Hut T-shirt.

I can't tell you how much joy it brings me when I see him wearing one when we get back home. I know that we have passed our love of the region on to him. It's so important to have tradition and consistency in uncertain times. I will always be grateful to The Cherry Hut being an unchanging icon of the region, where my family can walk in and always feel like we are home.

Thank You

**Professor Scott W. Wagner**
**Justice and Safety Department**
**Columbus State Community College**
**Columbus, OH 43215**

Claudia C. Breland

**From Nancy Waltz:**

My first visit was in 1949 when I was 9 months old. My grandparents built our Crystal Lake cottage in 1936. Each year we spent our summers there. My grandmother took us to The Cherry Hut for lunch. Each summer my brother and I continue our Cherry Hut tradition. When CA friends come to visit, they are treated to meals here. I have sent a menu to a dear friend every summer since 1994, and she still has each one.

I have copied the cherry decorations in my own kitchen. My cherry collection has come from The Cherry Hut. When people ask where our cottage is, I always start with, "Near The Cherry Hut." Then they know. One Thanksgiving I had two pies shipped to my family as a surprise. I used to take three pies in my carry-on when I flew home to CA. Thank you for all the memories.

Nancy Waltz kitchen

Nancy Waltz and grandchildren

**From Robin Vatalaro**
**Grosse Pointe Park**

Dear Cherry Jerry (and Case Family) –

This photo of my daughters Natasha and Shea in their Cherry Hut T-shirts, was taken at Point Betsie in 2011.

Natasha's first restaurant visited ever (and this momentous occasion is recorded in her baby book), in the summer of 2000 was The Cherry Hut. She was 4 weeks old and sat in her car seat in an upside-down Cherry Hut highchair. She looked around, garnered plenty of attention, but did not eat any cherry pie that year.

Natasha and Shea, Point Betsie

Since that year, except last year when she was out west on college required class, she has eaten Cherry Hut cherry pie—multiple slices in fact—as we always get a daily pie while we're in Beulah, every single summer.

**Claudia C. Breland**

Her sister Shea, born in 2003, also has never missed a summer at The Cherry Hut. We often wonder if it's possible to OD on Cherry Hut cherry pie. Hasn't happened yet. We have fun family arguments about who gets the job of serving the pie. On the days that there are five us (until my husband arrives later in the week), cutting the pie into five equally sized pieces is very difficult! This generally prompts further friendly arguments about who is getting the largest slice.

I started visiting Beulah in the summer when I was 8 (I was born in 1967). I only missed one summer, in my early twenties when another vacation conflicted. My parents (now age 85) have never missed a summer since 1975. That's a lot of cherry pie. My mother's parents, who lived their entire lives in Illinois, also vacationed at Crystal Lake once (I think back in the '50s?).

We just booked our Crystal Lake rental for this summer, this past week. Can't wait to celebrate your 100th anniversary! I can already taste the pie. The first order of business is always to pick up the pie, *then* proceed to the house (priorities).

BTW, I still have my "Cherry Jerry for President, 2016" sticker hanging in my office (along w/ my Five Shores Brewing sticker).

• • • • • • • • • • • • • • • • • • • • • • • • • • • • • • • • • • • • • • • • • • • • • • • • • •

**From Margaret Burrows-Getz:**

The story I have is the wedding of our oldest daughter (now thirty-six) on Memorial Day weekend of 2010. She and her now husband, dislike cake and wanted Cherry Hut pies for their reception. My husband and our German Shepherd Dog drove up to Beulah mid May 2010 and purchased twenty-four pies. He drove them back to our Grand Rapids, MI, residence where I froze them. We then drove them in coolers with dry ice to Washington, DC, for the wedding. My cousin (a ceramic artist) made a special presentation plate for a pie at the reception at the Washington Arts Club. The staff reheated the pies and after moments of surprise by the guests they were mobbed getting pies out of the kitchen ... once people tasted the pie even non-pie fans were sold. It was fun to bring a favorite summer treat to a special event.

Have pie
will travel

The wedding pie

Wedding of Megan Getz

**Claudia C. Breland**

**From Mark Bower:**

The summer of 2015, my wife and I, along with our kids (fourteen and nine) and our travel gnome, Ralf, took a cross country road trip from NY to the Grand Canyon and back. We missed a bunch of the upper Midwest states as well as the Upper Peninsula of Michigan. In the summer of 2018, the family flew out to Utah and drove back to NY. We drove through Idaho, Montana, the Dakotas and through the northern parts of Minnesota, Wisconsin and Michigan. We wanted to climb Sleeping Bear Dunes and heard that the Cherry Festival was the best. Unfortunately, we just missed the festival but were treated to a great surprise of finding The Cherry Hut. After a great family meal (finished off with cherry pie of course), we grabbed some items from the store (a cherry pie for breakfast and the cherry sour candies were the biggest hit). We then headed over to the Cherry Bowl drive-in for some entertainment. Back at home in NY, we have often ordered cherry pie from The Cherry Hut to be shipped to us and we long to get back some day for the Cherry Festival and of course the best cherry pie and those cherry sour candies. Our visit to The Cherry Hut is such a fond memory of our cross-country journey. Happy 100 years! Included is a picture of our travel gnome, Ralf, with Cherry Jerry.

Bower family travel gnome

**From Molly Sawyer Hiller:**

The Cherry Hut has been a Sawyer family tradition for as long as I can remember. It was always the first stop we would make at the beginning of our family vacations to, "the most beautiful place on Earth," my mom would say. As of 2021, we are now on to the 5th generation of the Sawyers stopping for lunch and cherry pie from The Cherry Hut.

My grandparents, Billie and Walter Sawyer, born in 1902, were the first of our family to discover this roadside stand with the "best cherry pie either of them had ever tasted." My grandfather, we fondly called Grannie, was a small-town doctor in Hillsdale, and would travel to northern Michigan with his wife, "Nannie," and their son, my dad, during the Depression for an inexpensive small getaway. After serving in WWII, their trips up north became more frequent and so did their stops for some cherry pie.

My father attended the University of Michigan and during that time met my mom. They married, settled down and had four children. And this is where I come in.

We lived in Iowa for a few years and then settled in Wisconsin for most of my life. Each summer, they would pack up the family into the old white station wagon, named Stacie, and head for Michigan to get out of the city and relax for two weeks. The first stop was visiting both sets of grandparents in lower Michigan and then on to our family vacation at the Homestead in Glen Arbor. My dad would say as we loaded back into the car, "we are taking the scenic route." We would all groan knowing it was going to be a long drive, but the best part of that long drive, without air conditioning I might add, was the stop at The Cherry Hut. By this time in the 1960s, it was no longer a roadside stand, but a full sit-down restaurant. The waitresses in their red and white striped dresses topped with their starched white aprons, would take our orders. Every one of us knew exactly what we would be ordering, even before we arrived in the parking lot, as it was a topic discussed at length while driving. We always began with the amazing cherryade while my dad would read through the menu to see where all of the young staff were from and where they were going to school. We would all enjoy our lunch when it arrived, but we were saving the best for last, the warm cherry pie à la mode! Before getting back into the car, we would head to the side window of the building to watch a little of the pie-making process. I had never seen so many pies in my life!

As the years passed by and our family was aging and growing, the one thing that stayed the same was our trip to northern Michigan. We no longer stayed at the Homestead, but rented a house on Glen Lake, big enough to handle us

Sawyer Hiller family

all. And this is when the next generation of Cherry Hut lovers began. My parents had moved from Wisconsin to North Carolina, my oldest sister, her husband and daughter lived in Virginia, my other sister lived in New Hampshire teaching during the summer, my brother lived in Indiana with his wife and two children and I lived in Milwaukee, Wisconsin, with my husband and two children. Our family vacation always began the same way—lunch at The Cherry Hut. We would set our alarm clock for 4 a.m., so that we could be out the door into a pitch-black sky, making sure we would all roll into the parking lot around noon. We would meet under the white trellis out front with lots of hugs and laughter and of course the annual photograph. The orders were still the same, beginning with the cherryade and ending the meal with by now the infamous cherry pie à la mode.

Well, the years continued on and so did the tradition of returning to northern Michigan. Our daughter taught violin at Interlochen for seven years and my older sister permanently moved to Traverse City. Our love for nature, the beautiful beaches and crystal-clear water kept us coming back, each year making that now treasured stop at The Cherry Hut.

Sawyer Hiller family

As this world is ever changing and the special places come and go, the one constant we have always counted on, is our lunch gathering at The Cherry Hut. Our family is now without our loving parents, Mom and Dad, Mimi and Papa, but the tradition they started so many years ago and now generations, continues on.

We are now on to the fifth generation of Sawyers, with our first granddaughter, Clara, and another one on the way, to stop and dine at The Cherry Hut. A few changes have been made to the dining room, like the beautiful mural painted on the front wall, but the memories of the love, the laughter and the beginnings of a long-anticipated vacation, starting with a slice of cherry pie, will never be altered.

Congratulations on your 100th year!!! May our traditions continue with you for the next 100 years.

**From Julie O'Brian:**

My family made our first visit to The Cherry Hut in 1962 when the "hut" was so much smaller and included an uncovered outdoor space. The servers were all cheery cherry girls from local high schools and state universities. They spent the summer on the shore of Crystal Lake when not bustling around the many visitors that made the intentional Cherry Hut stop. We had a regular routine leaving the Detroit area in the early hours stopping at Claire for a leisurely lunch and with renewed energy bound our way to Crystal Lake by midafternoon. We ate often at The Cherry Hut and no matter what we chose from the incredible menu of dishes starring the locally grown sweet and its cousin Montmorency cherry, the meal concluded with cherry pie and of course it was à la mode!

From the cherry wallpaper and cherry window valances to the red and white cherry uniforms the servers wore along with black and white saddle shoes to the cherry red carpet and smiling Cherry Jerry along US 31 lifelong memories have been made. And though 60 years have passed The Cherry Hut has remained a vibrant, close to our hearts destination any time we are up north, which thankfully is often! The pie, the cherry cola, the smiling cherry menu and Gwen Frostic place mats all have endeared this place along the clear waters of Crystal Lake to our hearts and we will always stop in to say "hello" as long as God wills and the "Hut" remains. Happy 100 years cherry Jerry and all The Cherry Hut gang! Cherry on.

**From Susan Ransom Firth:**

Congratulations on your 100 years! Our family has been coming off and on to Glen Arbor for 4 generations and we are bringing the 5th generation up this July to show her why we love it and also so my siblings and I can be in Benzonia to visit The Cherry Hut for your 100th year. My grandparents started visiting from their home in Glencoe, IL. I suspect our grandmother might have been there even before that with her parents. Our mother loved coming to Crystal Lake and Glen Lake with her parents and continued to spend several weeks there until she passed away. When our parents brought us to Crystal Lake and Glen Lake, we all remember getting to have lunch at The Cherry Hut and Mom would stock up on the jams and jellies to take home. As we've all made our way to the area, the vacations always include at least one visit and shipping or driving home goodies. I have a round menu from 2011 in the house and I'm pretty sure I have an older one somewhere. I couldn't wait to bring my kids to the area and now our granddaughter in July. We'll show her Glen Lake, Crystal Lake, Sleeping Bear Dunes and The Cherry Hut because all of those places hold memories. All four of us siblings wanted to come for the 100th and getting all of the family in one place is not easy so July will be especially fun. My sister is probably the best person to interview as she has been the sibling lucky enough to be a consistent visitor as she lives in Chicago. If you would like to interview her, please let me know.

**Again, congratulations!**
**Susan Ransom Firth**
**Charlotte, NC**

· · · · · · · · · · · · · · · · · · · · · · · · · · · · · · · · · · · · · · · · · · · · · · · · · · · · · · · · · · · ·

**From Heather Prestia Urban:**

My family purchased our vacation property in 1971. This is the year we started frequenting The Cherry Hut. One of my fondest memories of The Cherry Hut was when I was very young—maybe four years old. I would get my PJs on and we would all head to The Cherry Hut for dessert! It was always a cherry sundae for me! We would gather everyone—grandparents, uncles, aunts, and anyone who may have been staying with us! I'm happy to report that I carried this tradition on with my own kids who are in college now! I can only hope to be blessed to share in this tradition in the future if I am blessed with my own grandchildren! My family have been loyal patrons of The Cherry Hut for four generations! I hope that Cherry Hut will still be there for more generations to come!

· · · · · · · · · · · · · · · · · · · · · · · · · · · · · · · · · · · · · · · · · · · · · · · · · · · · · · · · · · · ·

**From Bill Burget:**

It started in the early 1960s. Some of the roads leading to Beulah from Columbus, Ohio, still consisted of billowing clouds of gravel. No one can remember who came up with the idea of the game but it probably was one of my parents seeking to occupy the time and attention of five kids and keeping them from their inevitable question of, "How much farther until we're there?"

The goal of the game was which of the five kids could first spot the very distinctive, red Cherry Hut signs posted along the roads of central and northwest Michigan leading to Beulah. Whoever was the first to spot a Cherry Jerry sign and yell out, "I see a Cherry Hut sign" got one point. Whoever spotted the most signs as we arrived at the restaurant in Beulah won the game. No prizes were awarded. Just beating your other four siblings was reward enough! A point was deducted if one of us, out of the very real fear of getting beat, mistakenly and prematurely yelled out, "I see a Cherry Hut sign," only to find out the squatty, rounded sign turned out to be a stop sign.

Pity my poor sisters who had the far back seat in the old Dodge station wagon where the seats faced backward! I also felt sorry for both my parents who suffered through five pairs of eyes glued to the front windshield, not knowing when the next observational outburst was screamed in their ears. We kids seemed to believe the volume of the scream was more important than being the first to scream. Not so. This game went on for years. Now, as we all still journey to Beulah—more individually as we've gotten older, rather than collectively—that big, red welcoming face of Cherry Jerry still brings a smile to our faces and an urge to again yell out, "I see The Cherry Hut sign!"

• • • • • • • • • • • • • • • • • • • • • • • • • • • • • • • • • • • • • • • • • • • • • • • • • • • • •

**From Anne Huffman Gilmore:**

My husband and I were married in my father's backyard in Manistee, Michigan, on October 5, 2019. When we were planning the wedding, and we got to the cake part, we knew exactly what we wanted. Cherry Hut cherry pie.

Anne Huffman
and Erik Gilmore

It's a staple of ours every time we visit over the Fourth of July and every other chance we get. We called and set up a large order a few months prior, and then the day of, friends drove up and picked up twenty cherry pies and ten apple that they had available that day.

Our guests LOVED it. Many of them were familiar with The Cherry Hut and giggled when it was served. And the family and friends that weren't familiar became big fans that day.

Now, on top of still enjoying Cherry Hut every time we visit, we now get to relive our wedding memories.

• • • • • • • • • • • • • • • • • • • • • • • • • • • • • • • • • • • • • • • • • • • • • • • • • • • • • •

**From Edith Taylor Molumby:**

I have been coming to The Cherry Hut for over seventy years—when it was just outside dining—first with my parents, grandparents, and siblings; then with my husband; then with our children; and now with our grandchildren who are the fifth generation of our family to eat at The Cherry Hut, as well as my siblings, their children and grandchildren, and extended family members.

In the 1950s, when it was all outside dining, my parents would ask my younger brother to count the fenceposts surrounding the eating area which would occupy him while waiting for his meal. We would often sit at the smaller children's tables outside next to our parents' larger table.

Also, in the 1950s, my parents bought my sister and me Cherry Hut dolls wearing Cherry Hut uniforms and with hair color which matched ours—one brunette and one auburn. I gave my Cherry Hut doll to Brenda Case to add to the Case family Cherry Hut memorabilia.

For many years we have brought pies back home to friends and neighbors. We still have a large Cherry Hut metal pie tin which would transport at least four pies back home safely in the car.

I wish you many more years of memories and continued success and I look forward to celebrating your 100th anniversary in the summer of 2022.

**From Carolyn Osborn Bowers:**

I worked at the Hut two summers when next door George ran the business part of Petritz Pies. Althea and another woman managed at the restaurant. I can see her in my mind but cannot recall her name. Memories of George running over to grab umbrellas in windstorms.

I had a friend whose cottage was close to the north end of Center Street. We would swim back and forth almost every morning between our cottage and her cottage. I would see The Cherry Hut sign and one day I decided to go ask about working at the Hut for the next summer. I was twelve years old; almost thirteen. One day I just got out of the water and walked over to ask who I would see about working next summer. Mrs. Petritz politely directed me to see Mr. Petritz at the building next door. I walked over and had a lovely conversation with Mr. Petritz. I told him where our cottage was on the corner of First and Center, that we come for the entire summer, that we lived in Mt. Pleasant, and this summer my brother and me were working together to purchase a figurine by Muriel Trapp for our mother for Christmas. He asked how old I was, and I told him I would be thirteen in September and my brother was two years older. He said that he would hire me if I had approval from my mother. I am sure he did not think I would ever show up in the spring and they had a chuckle over dinner that night. But I did show up letter in hand from Mom. So, they trained me, I passed and got the uniform and some shoes, made lots of friends and loved every minute of it.

One memory: There were a group of "ladies" that was always waited on by the managers because they were charming but difficult. We always passed the word that "the ladies from Frankfort" were coming. One time, one of the women asked if she could speak with me. She wanted to know if she could adopt me. We were speechless. I think I finally said I am working because it is fun and that my parents had to give them permission to let me work, but I was almost thirteen by then. I cannot remember if I said, "Thank you but I have a family."

We had a great group of people working together. Leonard was a dishwasher then. I thought it terrific that he became an owner and I enjoy seeing all the familiar folks doing sales behind the counter. Hopefully I will have a month Up North this summer.

Both of our children worked at the Hut while in college. Kate as a waitress, attending Miami University in Oxford, Ohio. David was a pie baker, attending Ohio State University. He did not mind getting up early to start the pie baking. One time when two people a row did not make it in to work, he came home after baking all day and announced that he set a huge record for number of pies baked in one day. His Cherry Hut team also won the build a raft and race it during a Fourth of July. I think there is still a small trophy in our bunk room; it just goes with the decor.

We still own our cottage at 2 South Center St. in Beulah. It is a family cottage with ownership with our children, and I hope to be able to spend more time there this summer.

My order of jams and jellies for Christmas was appreciated by all.

• • • • • • • • • • • • • • • • • • • • • • • • • • • • • • • • • • • • • • • • • • • • • • • • • • • • •

**From Ruth Potter:**

I turned eighty-six recently, so I have lots of memories of The Cherry Hut, but really not any one particular visit. What I remember is the stand on the highway and stopping to get a cherry pie to take to the cottage. I had forgotten about the outside tables until I saw the picture, then I remembered them vividly. We all would sit down and have your cherry drink! We always got some of your yummy jelly, too. Then later years the inside seating was added, then expanded. With the pandemic I still don't eat inside restaurants (I'm missing two-thirds of my right lung), but I did stop by last summer and got a couple of turkey pot pies to go! Also, a cherry pie.

• • • • • • • • • • • • • • • • • • • • • • • • • • • • • • • • • • • • • • • • • • • • • • • • • • • • •

**From Jane Sutherland:**

My parents were married in 1924, and spent several years after that at Van Demon's resort in Beulah on the lake, always visiting The Cherry Hut when they were there. Years later during World War II our family, which then included my older sister and I, went back to Van Demons for our vacations. This was 1942 and 1943, and I was a little girl who walked the one mile to town, most days, always going to The Cherry Hut for a piece of pie.

There was no gas available for private cars during the war, so one year we rode a very old-fashioned train to get there, open windows, cinders flying, straight back seats, and an open area in the rear, similar to photos of Abraham Lincoln campaigning. We returned home on the same train with my mother carrying a precious Cherry Hut pie on her lap the whole trip.

**Claudia C. Breland**

After about fifty years, I was finally able to take my husband to The Cherry Hut. By then it was a real restaurant, and the photos all around the room were exactly the way I remembered it from my childhood and the pie was just as good!

We now live in a retirement community in Massachusetts, and lo and behold there was a man living here who owned a cottage on Crystal Lake. He sadly has passed away, but he had a Cherry Jerry on his apartment door, and we shared many memories of The Cherry Hut.

It has been a happy part of my life for about 80 years, so thank you for keeping it alive and well, and congratulations on the 100th birthday.

Regards,

**Jane Sutherland**
**North Andover, MA**

• • • • • • • • • • • • • • • • • • • • • • • • • • • • • • • • • • • • • • • • • • • • • • • • • • • • • • • • • • • •

**From Pam Berke:**

My grandfather, Edward Gaul, was born and raised in Frankfort, MI. After he established his medical practice in Evansville, IN, he started taking his family back to MI over summers, and they stayed with friends on Crystal Lake. The first photo is of his children in 1953: Judy (eight), Jeff (one) and Joe (twelve). In 1957, he had a cottage built on the south shore of Crystal Lake. For nearly twenty years, the family gathered there every summer, building fond memories.

In the years since, his children and grandchildren have continued the tradition of visiting Crystal Lake, Frankfort, Beulah and of course, The Cherry Hut! In 2011, Joe organized a wonderful family reunion for a week in July. Judy, Jeff and Joe decided to recreate that photo in front of The Cherry Hut. I lost count of how many cherry pies our family carried out that week! In July 2022, we will gather once again, and Joe's son, Mark, is leading the charge this time for another family reunion extraordinaire.

Berke siblings in 1953: Judy, Jeff and Joe

Berke siblings in 2011

**Claudia C. Breland**

**From Sarah Gendich:**

Hello! This is my five-year-old son Jack! He's the fourth generation to continuously visit The Cherry Hut! We are from Rochester Hills and every Fourth of July we go to Crystal Lake and The Cherry Hut is a MUST every time we are in town. We couldn't imagine a Crystal Lake trip without it!

Jack Gendich 4th generation

Cherry Hut wishes Bobby & Kenny a Happy Birthday!

Cherry Hut Tradition! Three generations of Bob Etchen family, with his cousin Kenny Iverson. All traveling from Ohio, North Dakota, Florida and Traverse City.

Celebrating Bob's eightieth and Kenny's eighty-third birthdays!

They both have been coming to The Cherry Hut since they were five and eight years old! When they had cottages on Platte Lake. It has been a yearly destination all these years!

It all started with Bob and Kenny's grandparents and parents traveling from Platte Lake to pick up Cherry Hut pies in 1922 when they first opened!

**From Bob Jurczak:**

My story: My family and I are from Dyer, Indiana, and for vacations fished at Portage Lake. While I was four to five years old, I didn't like fishing and enjoyed our dinners every two days going to Cherry Hut and being surrounded with my family and enjoying your open face turkey sandwich dish and cherry pie! Thank you for this great 100-year book idea! I think that was just AWESOME!

**Sincerely,**
**Brian Jurczak**
**Kristin, Brian, Blake, Brooke, Ben Jurczak**

Cherry Hut baker

The Jurczak family: Kristin, Brian, Blake, Brooke and Ben

Blake Jurczak in 2013

**Claudia C. Breland**

**From Bob Bawell:**

Hi Cherry Jerry (Andy?),

Here are a few photos from the archives. Started coming to Crystal Lake in the early 1960s and was away for forty years. I was very happy to see my memories were still intact during my return visit in August 2010. You and your family are doing a great job, changing with the times but not too much. If you would like to use the attached photos you have my permission.

Best Regards,

**Bob Bawell
St. Louis, MO**

Bob Bawell
in 1960s

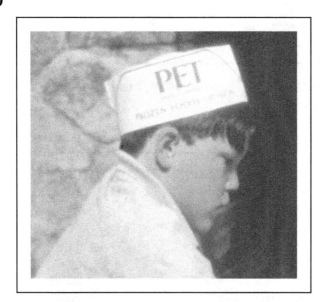

Cherry Hut
in the 1960s

Cherry Hut 1960s

Bob Bawell family in the 1960s

**Claudia C. Breland**

# Acknowledgments

**More than any of the other books I've written,** this was truly a group effort. I would like to thank the following for their contributions:

- Andy Case, owner and manager of The Cherry Hut, for taking me up on my offer to write the history, and for boxing up and sending me his entire archival collection. That box must have weighed forty pounds!
- Executive director Barbara Mort and board member Larry White, of the Benzie Area Historical Museum, for sharing their archives, which included the scrapbook put together by Ned Edwards and Mary Lonn (Trapp) King, and for connecting me with their publisher, Mission Point Press.
- Anne Stanton and Doug Weaver of Mission Point Press.
- The Reverend Ned Wolfe Edwards for sharing his memories of working at The Cherry Hut in the 1950s.
- Althea Kraker Petritz and her daughter Mimi Appel and A.J. Rogers III for sharing photographs and memories, and the many customers and staff members who were so generous in sharing memories and photographs!

## Photo credits

All the photos in this book were used with permission, and came from these collections:

- Claudia C. Breland personal archives
- Benzie Area Historical Museum
- Cherry Hut archives
- Althea Kraker Petritz personal archives
- A.J. Rogers III personal archives
- Personal archives of customers who shared their memories

# About the Author

**On November 4, 1954,** Mr. and Mrs. Maurice Reed (owners of Reedcraft Weavers, two doors down from The Cherry Hut) had a small announcement in the paper:

> Mr. and Mrs. Maurice Reed report the arrival of a little granddaughter, Claudia Catherine, born November 1 to Lt. and Mrs. John Chase Reed, who are now stationed at Albuquerque, New Mexico.

Claudia Reed birth announcement

Although she has never actually lived in Michigan, Claudia Breland has been coming to Beulah since childhood. The daughter of John Chase and Mary Reed, and granddaughter of Maurice and Ruby Reed, she fell in love with Benzie County at an early age. After Maurice Reed's death in 1971, Claudia received the file folders of family trees, typewritten stories, letters, newspaper clippings, and birth, marriage and death certificates, which sparked a lifelong passion for family history and genealogy.

She became a professional genealogist in 2009 and has had clients from around the world, having lectured in western Washington, Canada and at the National Genealogical Society conference. She is an avid user of DNA and has solved over twenty-five cases of unknown parent and grandparent puzzles. Claudia recently broke a forty-five-year brick wall, using DNA genetic networks, finding a black sheep second great-grandfather who deserted during the Civil War, and discovering a motive for murder in the death of her second great-grandmother in 1883. This is her sixth book.

## Previous books:

*Genealogy offline: a guide to family history records that are not online*
*Searching for your ancestors in historic newspapers*
*At home in Lansing: the journals of Maurice L. Reed, 1927-1931*
*Lansing and beyond: the journals of Maurice L. Reed, 1932-1934*
*On the Banks of the Pee Dee: the ancestry of Mary Gladys Jordan Sells*

**E-mail: ccbreland@comcast.net**
**Website: http://www.ccbreland.com**

# Source List

*The 1943 Flight Jacket Yearbook*, U.S. Navy: Pensacola, FL, 1943.

"600,000 Frozen Cherry Pies," *American Fruit Grower* (December 1948): 15. *Internet Archive* https://archive.org/details/sim_american-fruit-grower_1948-12_67_12/page/n1/mode/2up: 2021.

Brawley, Peggy. "Good Food: an interview with Jane and Michael Stern." *People* magazine (1 July 1983): 65.

Breland Research Files. Privately held by Claudia C. Breland [e-address for private use], Gig Harbor, Washington.

Brown, Virginia. "Cherry Pie – ½ Mile," *Farm Journal* 72 (June 1948): 94-95. *Internet Archive*. https://archive.org/details/sim_farm-journal_1948-06_72_6: 2021.

Call, Warren. Traverse City, Michigan. Interview by Claudia Breland, 1 February 2022. Notes, privately held by interviewer [address for private use], Gig Harbor, Washington.

Cherry Hut Menus. Cherry Hut Archives, 1922-2022. The Cherry Hut, Beulah, Michigan.

*Cherry Hut Scrapbook*. Benzonia Area Historical Museum, Benzonia, Michigan.

*Cherry Marketing Institute*. http://www.usacherries.com. 2022.

"The Coming Evolution in Orchard Machinery." *American Fruit Grower* (December 1948): 12-14. *Internet Archive* https://archive.org/details/sim_american-fruit-grower_1948-12_67_12/page/n1/mode/2up: 2021.

"Florida Marriages, 1830-1993." Database and images. http://www.familysearch.org/search/collection/1803936: 2021.

Florida. Orlando. *Orlando Evening Star*. 12 May 1967. Digital images. *Newspapers.com*. http://www.newspapers.com.

Florida. Orlando. *Orlando Sentinel*, 27 May 1973. Digital images. *Newspapers.com*. http://www.newspapers.com.

Gleason, Roberta. "Park Forest Singers take musical trip to Interlochen." *Southtown Star* (Tinley Park, IL), 6 August 1989: 43.

Hawaii. Hawaii County. *Hawaii (HI) Tribune-Herald*. 11 October 1955. Digital images. *Newspapers.com*. http://www.newspapers.com.

Hawaii. Honolulu. *Honolulu (HI) Advertiser*. 16 October 1955. Digital image. *Newspapers.com*. http://www.newspapers.com.

"If it's July, it must be time for those golden Rainier cherries," *The Christian Science Monitor*. https://www.csmonitor.com/2005/0706/p12s01-lifo.html. 2005.

Illinois. Chicago. *Chicago (IL) Tribune*. 25 November 1930. Digital images. *Newspapers.com*. http://www.newspapers.com.

Indiana. Indianapolis. *Indianapolis (IN) Star*. 25 August 2002. Cherry Hut archives, Beulah, Mich.

Indiana. South Bend. *South Bend (IN) Tribune*. Various issues. Digital images. *Newspapers.com*. http://www.newspapers.com.

Iowa. Des Moines. *Des Moines (IA) Register*. 5 April 1945. Digital image. *Newspapers.com*. http://www.newspapers.com.

Kraker, D.R. and J.L. "Selling Cherries in Pie Packages." *The Rural New Yorker* 85 (22 May 1926). *Internet Archive*. https://archive.org/details/ruralnewyorker85: 2019.

*Michigan: A Guide to the Wolverine State*, New York: Oxford University Press, 1941.

Michigan. Bay City. *Bay City (MI) Times*. Various issues. Digital images. *Newspapers.com*.
  http://www.newspapers.com.

Michigan. Benzie County. *Benzie (MI) Banner*. Various issues. Digital images. *Benzie Shores District Library*
  Newspapers collection. http://benzieshoreslibrary.org/Pages/Index/91099/newspaper-archive.

Michigan. Benzie County. *Benzie County (MI) Ad-Visor*. 25 July 1978. Digital images. *Benzie Shores District
  Library* Newspapers collection. http://benzieshoreslibrary.org/Pages/Index/91099/newspaper-
  archive.

Michigan. Benzie County. *Benzie County (MI) Patriot*. Various issues. Digital images. *Benzie Shores District
  Library* Newspapers collection. http://benzieshoreslibrary.org/Pages/Index/91099/newspaper-
  archive.

Michigan. Benzie County. *Benzie County (MI) Record Patriot*. Various issues. Digital images. *Benzie
  Shores District Library* Newspapers collection. http://benzieshoreslibrary.org/Pages/Index/91099/
  newspaper-archive.

Michigan. Benzie County. *Benzie (MI) Record*. Various issues. Digital images. *Benzie Shores District Library*
  Newspapers collection. http://benzieshoreslibrary.org/Pages/Index/91099/newspaper-archive.

Michigan. Benzie County. 1920 U.S. census, population schedule. Digital images, *Ancestry*.
  http://www.ancestry.com.

Michigan. Benzie County. "Deed Records, 1854-1923," Register of Deeds Office, Beulah.

Michigan. Berrien. *Benton Harbor (MI) Herald-Palladium*. Various issues. Digital images. *Newspapers.com*.
  http://www.newspapers.com.

Michigan. Berrien. *Saint Joseph (MI) Herald-Press*. Various issues. Digital images. *Newspapers.com*.
  http://www.newspapers.com.

Michigan. Calhoun. *Battle Creek (MI) Enquirer*. Various issues. Digital images. *Newspapers.com*.
  http://www.newspapers.com.

"Michigan cherry growers call 'checkmate' on Turkey imports." *Michigan Farm News*.
  http://www.michiganfarmnews.com/michigan-cherry-growers-call-checkmate-on-turkey-imports#:
  January 2021.

Michigan. Delta. *Escanaba (MI) Daily Press*. Various issues. Digital images. *Newspapers.com*.
  http://www.newspapers.com.

Michigan. Emmet. *Petoskey (MI) News-Review*. Various issues. Digital images. *Newspapers.com*.
  http://www.newspapers.com.

Michigan. Grand Traverse. *Traverse City (MI) Record-Eagle*. Various issues. Digital images.
  *Newspapers.com*. http://www.newspapers.com.

Michigan. Ingham. *Lansing (MI) State Journal*. Various issues. Digital images. *Newspapers.com*.
  http://www.newspapers.com.

Michigan. Leelanau. 1860 U.S. census, population schedules. Digital images. *Ancestry*.
  http://www.ancestry.com.

Michigan. Leelanau. *Leelanau (MI) Enterprise*. 3 June 1948. Digital image. *Newspapers.com*.
  http://www.newspapers.com.

Michigan. Kent County. *Grand Rapids (MI) Press*. Various issues. Digital images. *Genealogybank*.
  http://www.genealogybank.com.

Michigan. Mason. *Ludington (MI) Daily News*. 16 March 1931. Digital images. *Newspapers.com*.
  http://www.newspapers.com.

Michigan. St. Clair. *Port Huron (MI) Times Herald*. Various issues. Digital images. *Newspapers.com*. http://www.newspapers.com.

Michigan. Wayne. *Detroit (MI) Free Press*. Various issues. Digital images. *Newspapers.com*. http://www.newspapers.com.

Michigan State College, *The Record: Spartan Alumni Magazine,* 20 November 1951.

Moyer, Neva Ackerman. "This is the Life!" *Redbook* magazine (May 1951): 42-45. *Internet Archive*. https://archive.org/details/sim_redbook_1951-05_97_1/ : 2021.

*National Cherry Festival*. "History of Cherries." https://www.cherryfestival.org/p/get-cherries/ history-of-cherries. 2022.

New York. Ithaca County. *Class Book for 1912*, Cornell University, database and images. "U.S. School Yearbooks, 1900-1999," *Ancestry* http://www.ancestry.com: 2010.

New York. Jefferson. *Watertown (NY) Daily Times*. 11 February 1950. Digital image. *NYS Historic Newspapers*. http://nyshistoricnewspapers.org.

New York. New York. 1900 U.S. census, population schedule. Digital images, *Ancestry*. http://www.ancestry.com.

New York. New York. *New York Times*. Various issues. Cherry Hut archives, Beulah, Mich.

New York. New York. *Wall Street Journal*. 30 March 1992. Cherry Hut archives, Beulah, Mich.

New York. Ulster. *Kingston (NY) Daily Freeman*. 28 August 1941. Digital image. *NYS Historic Newspapers*. http://nyshistoricnewspapers.org.

*Open Corporates*. "Traverse City Canning Company." https://opencorporates.com/companies/us_mi/ 800057746. 2022.

*The Pet-Ritz Story*, St. Louis, MO: Pet Milk Company, 1959.

Petritz, Althea (Kraker). Traverse City, Michigan. Interview by Claudia Breland, various dates. Notes, privately held by interviewer [address for private use], Gig Harbor, Washington.

Reed, Percy. "Life Story of Percy A. Reed," 1947. Privately held by Claudia Breland [address for private use]. Gig Harbor, Washington.

Shipman, Viola. *The Recipe Box*, Farmington Hills, Mich.: Thorndike Press, 2018.

"St. Andrews History." *St. Andrews Presbyterian Church* (https://benziestandrews.com/about/ st-andrews-history/. 2022.

*The Traverse Region Historical and Descriptive*. Chicago: H.R. Page & Co., 1884.

*Stat News*. "First Covid-19 outbreak in a U.S. nursing home raises concerns." https://www.statnews.com/2020/02/29/ new-covid-19-death-raises-concerns-about-virus-spread-in-nursing-homes: 2021.

Stoddard, Veronica Gould. "10 great places to eat pie." *USA Today*. (27 August 1999): 3D.

*The Unofficial National Cherry Homepage*. "Cherry History in northern Michigan." http://www.leelanau.com/cherry/history.html. 2022.

Van Hammen, Rick. Honor, Michigan. Interview by Claudia Breland, 1 February 2022. Notes, privately held by interviewer [address for private use]. Gig Harbor, Washington.

Wait, S.E., compiler. *Old settlers: a historical and chronological record, together with personal experiences and reminiscences of members of the Old Settlers of the Grand Traverse region*. N.P.: Traverse City, MI, 1918.

Washington. King. *Seattle (WA) Times*. 4 January 2020. PDF Download, *ProQuest Library Database* (accessed from public library).

Winchell, Alexander. *The Grand Traverse Region*. Ann Arbor: Dr. Chase, 1866.

Wisconsin. Milwaukee County. 1900 U.S. census, population schedule. Digital images, *Ancestry*. http://www.ancestry.com.

Wisconsin. Milwaukee County. Marriages, 1838-1911. Database with images, "Milwaukee, Wisconsin, U.S. Marriages, 1838-1911." *Ancestry*. http://www.ancestry.com: 2018.

"World War II Draft Registration Cards." Database with images. *Fold3*. https://www.fold3.com/image/671916966: 2012.

# Endnotes

1   1900 U.S. census, Milwaukee Co. WI, pop. sched., Milwaukee, ED 14, p.11, dwelling 196, family 2017, Augustus J. Rogers household; citing NARA microfilm T623, roll 1800.

2   "Milwaukee, Wisconsin, U.S., Marriages, 1838-1911," *Ancestry* > 1902 > 142-144 > image 652 of 753; Milwaukee, WI Marriage Book for 1902, p.305, no. 1421, Rogers-Passmore (1902).

3   "VanDeman's Land," *Benzie (Mich.) Banner*, 21 July 1904, p.4, col. 2; digital image, *Benzie Shores District Library* (http://www.benzieshoreslibrary.org). This item probably referred to Dorothy's brother, A.J. Rogers Jr.

4   "All Over Benzie County," *Benzie (Mich.) Record*, 1 September 1911, p.4, col. 2; digital image, *Benzie Shores District Library* (http://www.benzieshoreslibrary.org).

5   Althea (Kraker) Petritz (Traverse City, Michigan), interview by Claudia C. Breland, 28 January 2022; notes privately held by interviewer, Gig Harbor, Washington, 2022.

6   1900 U.S. census, New York Co., NY, pop. sched., Manhattan, ED 619, p.17, dwell. 113, fam. 351, Sophia Kraker household; citing NARA microfilm T623, roll 1108.

7   "U.S. School Yearbooks, 1900-1999," *Ancestry* > New York > Ithaca > Cornell University > 1912 > image 789 of 1220; *Cornell Class Book for 1912*, p.162, James Lewis Kraker.

8   Althea (Kraker) Petritz, interview, 28 January 2022.

9   "Marriage Licenses," *Benzie Banner*, 30 August 1917, p.2, col. 5.

10  1920 U.S. census, Benzie Co., Mich., population schedule, Benzonia, enumeration district (ED) 2, p.2A, dwelling 34, family 35, James L. Kraker household; citing NARA microfilm T625, roll 756. Also, Benzie County, Mich. Register of Deeds, 50:117, Percy and Mary Reed to James L. and Dorothy R. Kraker (1921).

11  Reed, Percy, "Life Story of Percy A. Reed," (typescript, ca. 1987), transcribed by Dorcas Small Humphrey, p.12; copy in possession of Claudia C. Breland [Address for Private Use], Gig Harbor, WA, 2021.

12  "Agricultural Agent Appointed for Benzie Co.," *Benzie Banner*, 16 January 1919, p.1, col. 3.

13  Virginia Brown, "Cherry Pie—½ Mile," *Farm Journal*, v.72, issue 6 (June 1948), p.94; PDF download, *Internet Archive* (http://www.archive.org: accessed 10 December 2021).

14  "Northwest Region Plans Cherry Fete," *Detroit (Mich.) Free Press*, 23 March 1924, p.49, col. 6; digital image, *Newspapers.com* (http://www.newspapers.com).

15  "Making Plans for Blossom Festival," *Escanaba (Mich.) Daily Press,* 30 April 1925, p.1, col. 4; digital image, *Newspapers.com*. Also, "Grand Traverse to State Cherry Fete," *Saint Joseph (Mich.) Herald-Press*, 10 April 1924, p.3, col. 2; digital image, *Newspapers.com*. Also, "Traverse Will Select Cherry Queen Tonight," *Saint Joseph Herald-Press*, 13 July 1928, p.5, col. 7.

16  "Michigan Cherry Pie for President," *Port Huron (Mich.) Times Herald,* 17 August 1926, p.8, col. 5; digital image, *Newspapers.com*.

17  D.R. and J.L. Kraker, "Selling Cherries in Pie Packages," *The Rural New Yorker*, 22 May 1926, v.85 no. 4900, p.835; PDF download, *Internet Archive* (http://www.archive.org: accessed 5 January 2022).

18  Penny Misner, "Making mouthwatering cherry pies since 1927," *Benzie County Record Patriot*, 2 July 1997, p.10, col. 1; digital image, *Benzie Shores District Library* (http://www.benzieshoreslibrary.org).

19  "400 Attend Opening of Fruit Meet," *The Saint Joseph (Mich.) Herald-Press*, 4 March 1920, p.1, col. 6.

20  "Discuss Gd. Traverse Cherry Pool Project," *Benzie Banner*, 20 April 1920, p.1, col. 1. Also, Ned

Edwards, Beulah, Michigan [e-address for private use], to Claudia Breland, e-mail, 20 January 2022, "Reviewing your chapters," Breland Research Files: privately held by Breland [e-address for private use], Gig Harbor, Washington.

21  "Cherry Growers Held Meeting Tuesday Night," *Benzie Banner*, 15 June 1922, p.4, col. 3.

22  "County Agent Kraker Issues Public Statement Regarding Resignation," *Benzie Banner*, 6 March 1924, p.1, col. 1.

23  "Cherries Ripe," *Benzie Banner*, 18 June 1925, p.1. Note: the first two lines of this poem were taken from "Cherry-Ripe," by Robert Herrick, English poet (1591–1674).

24  "Roadside Market Sells 1,500 Pies," *Grand Rapids (Mich.) Press*, 4 November 1926, p.26, col.2.

25  "Cherry Pies at a Roadside Hut," *Traverse City (Mich.) Record-Eagle*, 15 July 1929, p.3, col. 3; digital image, *Newspapers.com*.

26  "Now Open on U.S. 31," *Benzie Banner*, 12 July 1928, p.6, col. 4.

27  "Cherry Hut for the Loop," *Chicago Tribune*, 25 November 1930, p.27, col. 8; digital image, *Newspapers.com*.

28  "Open 'Cherry Hut' in Chicago Loop District," *Benzie Banner*, 13 November 1930, p.1, col. 1.

29  "Local People Managing Cherry Hut in Chicago," *Benzie Banner*, 5 March 1932, p.1, col. 1.

30  Althea (Kraker) Petritz, interview, 4 February 2022.

31  "Finds Romance in Growing Cherries, Horticulturist Tells Mason Fruit Growers," *Ludington (Mich.) Daily News*, 16 March 1931, p.1, col. 7; digital image, *Newspapers.com*.

32  "Concrete Loop Thru Beulah Approved by State This Week," *Benzie Banner*, 21 July 1932, p.1, col. 1.

33  "Davis Quality Bakery," *Benzie Banner*, 21 July 1932, p.1, col. 5.

34  "Free Talking Pictures at Beulah Park Every Wednesday Night," *Benzie Record supplement*, 5 July 1934, p.3, header.

35  "Cherry Hut Will Open," *Benzie Record*, 27 June 1935, p.6, col. 3.

36  "Cherry Hut is Open Again," *Benzie Banner*, 8 July 1937, p.12, col. 3.

37  "Celery Growing Becomes Big Business in Beulah," *Escanaba (Mich.) Daily Press*, 23 August 1933, p.3, col. 6; digital image, *Newspapers.com*. Also, "Martin Trapp Dies at 86," *Benzie Record*, 23 August 1962, p.20, col. 3. Also, "The Crystal Gazer," *Benzie Banner*, 6 October 1949, p.2, col. 2.

38  *FamilySearch* (familysearch.org/search/catalog/238631) > Index to deeds v. B, ca. 1890-1923 > image 639 of 657, Martin Trapp from J.C. Desmond; Benzie County, Mich. Deed Index vol. B, n.p. (1920).

39  Edwards to Breland, 3 February 2022.

40  "Cherries Ripening Fast—Pickers to Receive Less Pay," *Benzie Banner*, 2 July 1931, p.1, col. 1.

41  "Cherry Picking Under Way in Benzie County," *Benzie Banner*, 14 July 1932, p.1, col. 2.

42  "Jobs Available for 5000 Cherry Pickers is Belief," *Benzie Banner*, 2 July 1936, p.1, col. 5.

43  "Cherry Fruit Fly Found at Beulah," *Benzie Banner*, 27 June 1946, p.1, col. 1.

44  "Estimates Half of Cherry Crop Killed by Frost," *Benzie Banner*, 28 April 1938, p.1, col. 1.

45  "Benzie Resorts and Hotels Report Record 4th Week-End Business," *Benzie Banner*, 9 July 1936, p.1, col. 1. Also, "Vacation Land Greets Those Pleasure Bent," *Traverse City Record-Eagle*, 30 June 1934, p.1, col. 8.

46  "Successful Benzie Resort Season Draws to a Close," *Benzie Banner*, 2 September 1937, p.1, col. 1.

47  "Slump-Proof Resorts: Traverse Section Sees Visitors Coming Early with Plans to Stay Late," *Bay City (Mich.) Times*, 5 July 1932, p.3, col. 1; digital image, *Newspapers.com*.

48  "A&P Food Stores," *Traverse City Record-Eagle*, 17 June 1932, p.9, col. 5.

49  Viola Shipman, *The Recipe Box*, (Farmington Hills, Mich.: Thorndike Press, 2018), p.226. Used with permission.

50  Althea (Kraker) Petritz, interview, 4 February 2022.

51  "No Sugar Rationing for Two Weeks," *Benzie Banner*, 19 March 1942, p.1, col. 4.

52  "Sugar Rationing Cards Must be Obtained by May 4, 5, or 6," *Benzie Banner*, 30 April 1942, p.1, col. 4.

53  "Sugar Rationing Now in Effect," *Benzie Banner*, 7 May 1942, p.1, col. 5.

54  Edwards to Breland, 20 January 2022.

55  "Benzie Fails in War Bond Sale," *Benzie Banner*, 22 April 1943, p.1, col. 1.

56  "Rationing at a Glance," Ibid.

57  "Sugar Permits for Canning Available," *Benzie Banner*, 11 June 1942, p.1, col. 4.

58  "Scholarships Given For Farm School," *Kingston (N.Y.) Daily Freeman*, 28 August 1941, p.1, col. 5; digital image, *NYS Historic Newspapers* (http://www.nyshistoricnewspapers.org).

59  "WWII Draft Registration Cards," database and images, *Fold3* (http://www.fold3.com: accessed 20 January 2022), James Lewis Kraker Jr., serial no. S-178,

60  *The 1943 Flight Jacket Yearbook*, (U.S. Navy: Pensacola, FL, 1943), p.97; digital image, *Fold3* (http://www.fold3.com: accessed 20 January 2022). Also, *FamilySearch* (familysearch.org/search/collection/1803936) > Florida Marriages, 1830-1993 > image 4922 of 5120, James Kraker and Dorothy Dodds (1943).

61  "James Kraker," *Benzie County Record Patriot*, 18 June 2013, digital image, (https://www.recordpatriot.com/news/article/James-Kraker-14312735.php: accessed 20 January 2022).

62  "Lt. Dexter Warren Reported Missing," *Benzie Banner*, 4 May 1944, p.1, col. 3.

63  "Free Men," *Traverse City Record-Eagle*, 24 May 1945, p.9, col. 6.

64  "Kraker-Petritz Nuptials Saturday," *Benzie Banner*, 10 October 1946, p.1, col. 5.

65  "George K. Petritz," *Benzie Record Patriot*, 29 December 2010, p.6, col. 2. Also, "Brother Lost – So Joe Went to Sea," *Des Moines (Iowa) Register*, 5 April 1945, p.9, col. 3; digital image, *Newspapers.com*.

66  "Two of 1,600 Escape; One is Lieut. Petritz," *South Bend (Ind.) Tribune*, 26 April 1945, p.1, col. 5; digital image, *Newspapers.com*.

67  Ibid.

68  "Leelanau Lookout," *Leelanau (Mich.) Enterprise*, 3 June 1948, p.10, col. 4; digital image, *Central Michigan University, Clarke Historical Library, Digital Michigan Newspapers* (http://www.digmichnews.cmich.edu).

69  "600,000 Frozen Cherry Pies," *American Fruit Grower*, December 1948, p.15; PDF download, *Internet Archive* (http://www.archive.org: accessed 2 February 2022).

70  "Cherry Hut in Production of Xmas Gift Packages," *Benzie Banner*, 6 October 1949, p.12, col. 2. Also, Althea (Kraker) Petritz, interview, 4 February 2022.

71  Ibid.

72  1860 U.S. census, Leelanau Co., Mich., population schedule, Crystal Lake, p.825, dwelling & family 221, Lucius W. Case household; citing National Archives and Records Administration microfilm M653, roll 550. Also, "Impressions of the Man," *Benzie County Ad-Visor*, 25 July 1978, p.1, col. 1.

73  "Leonard Leach Case Jr.," *Benzie County Record Patriot* (https://www.recordpatriot.com/news/article/Leonard-Leach-Case-Jr-14322834.php: accessed 24 January 2022).

74 "Cherry Hut to Expand Facilities," *Benzie Banner*, 27 June 1946, p.16, col. 2.

75 "Esther Rockwell," *Benzie County (Mich.) Record Patriot*, 28 May 2014.

76 "Pie on the Fly," *Benzie Banner*, 25 July 1946, p.1, col. 1.

77 "Beulah's Pet-Ritz Cherry Pie Plant Nationally Publicized," *Benzie Banner*, 18 March 1948, p.12, col. 5.

78 "Pie for the President," *Benzie Banner*, 1 July 1948, p.1, col. 3.

79 "Dorothy Reed, Benzonia Sr., County Cherry Pie Champion," *Benzie Banner*, 6 February 1947, p.1, col. 1.

80 "Will Pick Winner in County Cherry Pie Baking Contest," *Benzie Banner*, 29 January 1948, p.1, col. 1.

81 Cherry Hut menu for 1948, Cherry Hut archives, Beulah, Mich.

82 "Cherry Hut Properties Bought by Petritz Foods; Krakers Leave for N.Y.," *Benzie Banner*, 2 February 1950, p.1, col. 1. Also, "Returns to Gouverneur," *Watertown (NY) Daily Times*, 11 February 1950, p.1, col. 8; digital image, *NYS Historic Newspapers* (http://www.nyshistoricnewspapers.org).

83 "Petritz Foods Buys Froz-N Foodbank," *Benzie Record*, 5 April 1951, p.1, col. 4. Also, "Sidelights," *Battle Creek (Mich.) Enquirer*, 26 August 1951, p.30, col. 4; digital image, *Newspapers.com*.

84 Neva Ackerman Moyer, "This is the Life!" *Redbook* magazine, May 1951, p.42; PDF download, *Internet Archive* (https://archive.org/details/sim_redbook_1951-05_97_1/page/n43/mode/2up: accessed 29 January 2022).

85 "Pet Milk Buys Two State Firms," *Lansing (Mich.) State Journal*, 29 September 1955, p.38, col. 4; digital image, *Newspapers.com*.

86 "Pet Milk Co. Buys Plants," *The Honolulu (Haw.) Advertiser*, 16 October 1955, p.11, col. 3; digital image, *Newspapers.com*. Also, "Pet Milk Co. Expands Its Operations," *Hawaii Tribune-Herald (Hilo, Hawaii)*, 11 October 1955, p.6, col. 6.

87 "The Pet-Ritz Story," (St. Louis, MO: Pet Milk Company, 1959), p.22.

88 "Cherry Picker Shortage Cited," *Lansing State Journal*, 17 July 1951, p.5, col. 2. Also, "Cherry Pickers Arrive," *Petoskey (Mich.) News-Review*, 16 July 1951, p.1, col. 4; digital image, *Newspapers.com*.

89 "No One is Alarmed at Population Drop," *Petoskey News-Review*, 22 August 1950, p.4, col. 2.

90 "Buying Cherries Day to Day Basis," *Benzie County Patriot*, 27 July 1950, p.3, col. 5.

91 "They Did It with Their Little Hatchets," *Saint Joseph Herald-Press*, 1 August 1950, p.6, col. 1.

92 Photographs of Mary Lonn Trapp, Cherry Hut Scrapbook, Benzie Historical Museum.

93 Edwards to Breland, 20 January 2022.

94 "Mary Lonn Trapp Chosen National Cherry Queen Over 23 Contestants," *Benzie Banner*, 5 July 1951, p.1, col. 1.

95 "Queen Relaxes Before Starting Reign," *Traverse City Record-Eagle*, 9 July 1951, p.1, col. 2. Also, "Queen Gets Her Crown," Ibid., 12 July 1951, p.1, col. 7. Also, "Meet the Cherry Queen," *Detroit Free Press*, 24 July 1951, p.2, col. 1.

96 "Mary Lonn Completes 10-Day Trip," *Benzie Banner*, 9 September 1951, p.1., col. 3.

97 "Spartan Alumni – 12,000 Strong Return for Homecoming Festivities," Michigan State College, *The Record: Spartan Alumni Magazine,* 20 November 1951, p.2, col. 1; PDF download, (https://projects.kora.matrix.msu.edu/files/162-565-907/19511120sm.pdf: accessed 28 January 2022).

98 "A lovely wedding…," *Benzie Record,* 6 September 1956, p.3, col. 1.

99 "St. Andrews History," web page, *St. Andrews Presbyterian Church* (https://benziestandrews.com/about/st-andrews-history/: accessed 2 February 2022).

100  Alexander Winchell, *The Grand Traverse Region* (Ann Arbor: Dr. Chase's Steam Printing House, 1866), p.75; PDF download, *Internet Archive* (http://www.archive.org: accessed 6 February 2022). This author's grandfather Maurice L. Reed attended Benzonia Academy.

101  Althea (Kraker) Petritz, interview, 28 January 2022.

102  "Receive School Honors," *Benzie Banner*, 9 April 1953, p.1, col. 5.

103  "Top Students," *Benzie Banner*, 3 March 1955, p.1, col. 1.

104  "Top Students," *Benzie Banner*, 18 March 1954, p.1, col. 3.

105  "Honor Students," *Traverse City Record-Eagle*, 20 March 1958, p.8, col. 4.

106  "Cherry is Our First Name," *New York Times,* 9 March 1958, p.XX8, col. 2; digital image, *ProQuest Historical Newspapers: The New York Times* (accessed from library database, 20 January 2022).

107  "Mrs. J. Kraker of Beulah Dies," *Traverse City Record-Eagle*, 5 May 1958, p.17, col. 1. Also, "Beulah Woman Dies Suddenly," *Benzie Record*, 8 May 1958, p.12, col. 5.

108  "Cherry Hut Has New Owner," *Benzie Record*, 25 June 1959, p.1, col. 3. Also, "Beulah Cherry Hut is Sold," *Traverse City Record-Eagle*, 19 June 1959, p.7, col. 1.

109  "James Kraker Taken by Death," *Traverse City Record-Eagle*, 1 August 1960, p.17, col. 4. Also, "Death Calls J.L. Kraker," *Benzie Banner,* 4 August 1960, p.16, col. 4.

110  "Chamber Fund Drive Near Goal," *Traverse City Record-Eagle,* 16 September 1961, p.3, col. 5. *Also,* "Beulah-Benzonia C-C Elects Officers," *Traverse City Record-Eagle*, 13 December 1962, p.30, col. 3.

111  Virginia Baird, "Look What's Coming in New Michigan Food Products!" *Lansing State Journal*, 3 June 1960, p.23, col. 1.

112  "Beulah Business Adds Facilities," *Traverse City Record-Eagle*, 13 July 1964, p.18, col. 4.

113  "Miscellaneous For Sale," *Traverse City Record-Eagle* 9 April 1964, p.22, col. 8.

114  "Benzie Man Buys Florida Business," *Traverse City Record-Eagle*, 16 May 1967, p.7 col. 4.

115  "Bulk Sales Notice," *Orlando (FL) Evening Star*, 12 May 1967, p.36, col. 7. Also, "Citrus Tower adds candy factory," *Orlando (FL) Sentinel*, 27 May 1973, p.233, col. 2.

116  "Guild Plans Spring Fantasy," *Lansing State Journal*, 26 April 1961, p.35, col. 1.

117  Leonard L. Case, "Art Activity Flourishes in Benzie Village," *Traverse City Record-Eagle*, 10 December 1966, p.7, col. 1.

118  "Okinawa Group Visits Benzie," *Traverse City Record-Eagle*, 2 May 1961, p.11, col. 2. Also, "Tiny Town Thrives on International Trade," *Grand Rapids (Mich.) Press*, 24 November 1966, p.45, col. 2.

119  Rick Van Hammen, Honor, Michigan, interview by Claudia Breland, 1 February 2022, notes privately held by interviewer, Gig Harbor, Washington, 2022.

120  "Restaurant, The Cherry Hut," *Grand Rapids Press*, 7 June 1969, p.27, col. 3.

121  Rick Van Hammen, interview, 1 February 2022.

122  "Engagement Announced," *Traverse City Record-Eagle,* 21 March 1972, p.10, col. 1.

123  "Repeats Nuptial Vows at Benzonia Church," *Traverse City Record-Eagle*, 24 June 1972, p.10, col. 2.

124  "National Coho Salmon Festival at Honor, Michigan," *Traverse City Record-Eagle*, 20 September 1972, p.19, col. 1.

125  "Benzie Co-Op To File for Bankruptcy," *Traverse City Record-Eagle*, 5 January 1972, p.14, col. 4.

126  "Beulah Couple to Observe 50th Anniversary," *Traverse City Record-Eagle*, 24 July 1959, p.24, col. 2.

127  "Dedication officially marks Sleeping Bear as National Park," *Benzie County Record Patriot*, 26 October 1977, p.1, col. 1.

128  Suzanne Harris, "Ugh! Too Much: Festival Influx Unexpected," *Benzie County Patriot*, 9 July 1975, p.1, col. 1.

129  Althea (Kraker) Petritz, interview, 4 February 2022.

130  "The Cherry Hut Restaurant," *Benzie County Record Patriot*, 5 September 1979, p.16, col. 1.

131  NR Waring, Ann Arbor, Michigan [e-address for private use] to Claudia Breland, e-mail, 11 December 2021, "Cherry Hut" Breland Research Files, privately held by Breland, Gig Harbor, Washington.

132  "Name Your favorites in Michigan eating," *Detroit Free Press*, 13 July 1983, p.27, col. 1.

133  Peggy Brawley, "Good Food: an interview with Jane and Michael Stern," *People* magazine, 1 July 1983, p.65.

134  "Michigan's Amazing Autumn," *Battle Creek Enquirer*, 25 September 1987, p.9, col. 1. Also, "Cherry Pie-Pickin' Time," *South Bend (Ind.) Tribune*, 13 February 1989, p.33, col. 1. Also, "Jerry a Cherry Hut fixture," *Benzie County Record Patriot*, 5 August 1987, section II, p.7.

135  Roberta Gleason, "Park Forest Singers take musical trip to Interlochen," *Southtown Star (Tinley Park, Ill.)*, 6 August 1989, p.43, col. 1; digital image, *Newspapers.com*.

136  Tom Northway, "Jerry a Cherry Hut fixture," *Benzie County Record Patriot*, 5 August 1987, section II, p.7, col. 1.

137  "History of 'Hut' rich in family involvement since 1922," *Benzie County Record Patriot*, 12 June 2002, section II, p.5.

138  Althea (Kraker) Petritz, interview, 4 February 2022.

139  Tom Northway, "Dried cherries stir excitement," *Benzie County Record Patriot*, 7 March 1984, p.3, col. 1.

140  Angela Haase, [e-address for private use], to Claudia Breland, e-mail, 29 January 2022, "For your Cherry Hut project," Breland Research Files: privately held by Breland [e-address for private use], Gig Harbor, Washington.

141  Cherry Hut ad, *Benzie County Record Patriot*, 30 May 1990, p.14, col. 2.

142  Cherry Hut ad, Ibid., 10 June 1992, p.25, col. 3.

143  Allison Engel, "Old-Fashioned Frugality is Back in Fashion," *The Wall Street Journal*, 30 March 1992.

144  Warren Call, Traverse City. Interview by Claudia Breland, 20 January 2022; notes privately held by interviewer, Gig Harbor, Washington, 2022.

145  "Cherries Jubilee: Mary Engelbreit uses her signature summer fruit to lure us all out of the winter doldrums," *South Bend (Ind.) Tribune*, 3 February 1997, p.25, col. 1.

146  Neal Rubin, "Have Olds, Will Travel: There's something to see in every Michigan county," *Detroit Free Press*, 13 January 1991, pp.1D & 4D.

147  Veronica Gould Stoddart, "10 great places to eat pie," *USA Today*, 27 August 1999, p.3D, col. 1. This was also printed in the *Battle Creek Enquirer*, 5 September 1999, p.59, col. 2.

148  Cherry Hut menus, 1968-2013, Cherry Hut archives, Beulah, Mich.

149  Call, interview, 20 January 2022.

150  R.W. Apple Jr., "Up North: Michigan's Flavorful Vacationland," *New York Times*, 30 July 2003, p.D1, col. 1.

151  R.W. Apple Jr., "In the Midwest, a Sweet Tooth is Nonpartisan," *New York Times*, 27 October 2004, p.D4, col. 1.

152  Greg Morago, "'Roadfood' celebrates 25 years of regional cuisine," *Lansing State Journal*, 24 November 2002, p.52, col. 1.

153  Lori Hall Steele, "Cherry farmers brace for worst," *Traverse City Record-Eagle*, 30 June 2002, p.1, col. 1.

154  Marisa Maldonado, "State cherry crop harvest at risk," *Detroit Free Press*, 6 July 2003, p.1, col. 4.

155  Robert Fitzke, "Cherry Hut marks its 90th," *Benzie County Record Patriot*, Summer Scene, 28 August 2012 (https://www.recordpatriot.com/summer-scene/article/Cherry-Hut-marks-its-90th-14327177.php: accessed 7 February 2022).

156  Edwards to Breland, e-mail, 3 February 2022.

157  John M. Flora, "Cherry Hut Built on Dessert," *Indianapolis Star*, 25 August 2002, section K.

158  "Leonard Leach Case, Jr.," *Benzie County Record Patriot*, April 2016 (https://www.recordpatriot.com/news/article/Leonard-Leach-Case-Jr-14322834.php: accessed 7 February 2022).

159  Edwards to Breland, e-mail, 3 February 2022.

160  "News," *Seattle (Wash.) Times*, 4 January 2020, p.A2.

161  "First Covid-19 outbreak in a U.S. nursing home raises concerns," *Stat News* (https://www.statnews.com/2020/02/29/new-covid-19-death-raises-concerns-about-virus-spread-in-nursing-homes/: accessed 25 January 2022).

162  Kristen Jordan Shamus, Eric D. Lawrence, "Virus Impact Hits Michigan," *Detroit Free Press*, 12 March 2020, p.A1, col. 1. Also, Paul Egan, Mark Kurlyandchik, "Bars, restaurants told to close," *Detroit Free Press*, 17 March 2020, p.A1, col. 1.

163  Andy Case, Beulah, Michigan. [e-address for private use], to Claudia Breland, e-mail, 24 January 2022, "Re: questions for you," Breland Research Files, privately held by Breland, Gig Harbor, Washington.

164  Rick Van Hammen, interview, 1 February 2022. These lugs are called 5 to 1 because they contain 25 pounds of cherries and 5 pounds of sugar.

165  The Marshall Turkey Farm was advertising in the *Benzie Banner* as early as 1929: "Benzie Turkeys for State Farm," *Benzie Banner*, 31 October 1929, p.1, col. 4. For the 1936 date, see Penny Misner, "Making mouthwatering cherry pies since 1927," *Benzie County Record Patriot*, 2 July 1997, p.10, col. 1.

166  Rick Van Hammen, interview, 1 February 2022. Also, Warren Call, interview, 20 January 2022.

167  Haase to Breland, e-mail, 29 January 2022.

CPSIA information can be obtained
at www.ICGtesting.com
Printed in the USA
JSHW041916170822
29378JS00004B/72